FROM IDEA TO PRODUCT/ MARKET FIT

AN INSPIRATIONAL STARTUP GUIDE TO TURN IDEAS INTO ACTION

FROM IDEA TO PRODUCT/ MARKET FIT

AN INSPIRATIONAL STARTUP GUIDE TO TURN IDEAS INTO ACTION

OMAR MOHOUT

First print: May 2017
Second print: October 2018
Third print: June 2019
Fourth print: September 2021

D/2017/0147/285
ISBN: 978 28 7403 460 2
Order number: 208 174 003

© 2021 die Keure Professional Publishing
Kleine Pathoekeweg 3
8000 Brugge
Tel.: (050) 47 12 72
Fax: (050) 33 51 54
E-mail: professional.publishing@diekeure.be
Website: www.diekeure.be

92637

Table of Contents

Exodus:
Problem / Solution Stage

Numeri:
Product / Market fit

Foreword

Kobe Verdonck, CEO SD Worx

The success of a company always lies in making things people want. Although this might sound trivial – it is far from easy to get this exactly right. As Omar points out in his book, "... it is much easier to expand from something that a small number of people love, to something that a lot of people love".

Successful companies are all about turning ideas into action quickly and efficiently. Taking action is the hard part. Even though it's common to say that ideas mean nothing and execution is everything, the reality is more nuanced. Even the world's best companies with incredible execution will fail if their idea is fundamentally flawed, or if the assumed market is too small. Innovation in this age of accelerating market speed is on the crossroad of people and technology. To rethink how people and tech work together now and in the future is a challenge for every business small or big.

In today's new world of work, people want to be inspired by what they do and have the freedom to focus on what matters. Organisations need a dynamic, motivated workforce empowered by smart technology to compete in this era of digitalisation, automatization and innovation. As a leading European provider of people solutions, SD Worx turns HR into a source of value for our customers' business and the people that work for them. After all, people always make the difference between good and great!

In short, just like this inspiring book, SD Worx provides companies with the tools they need to excel, innovate, transform and ultimately grow.

Enjoy the reading!

Introduction

Successful startups are all about turning ideas into action quickly and efficiently. Taking action is the hard part.

Entrepreneurs often come to us with ideas, asking for help and input on the next steps. This always seemed strange to me, since the steps are the same for any business. In fact, the magic is supposed to be in the idea.

Launching a startup requires the willingness to fail and learn. Avoiding failure is not a sign that you're smart and being smart is not about knowing all the answers; it's about being able to find them. While knowledge is about knowing the right answer, the intelligence is about asking the right questions.

Even though it's common for startups to say that ideas mean nothing and execution is everything, the reality is more nuanced. Even the world's best entrepreneurs with incredible execution will fail if their idea is fundamentally flawed, or if the assumed market is too small.

Achieving product/market fit is the transformative moment in the life of a startup. It's that moment when the offering aligns with market needs. Product/market fit is the magic moment when users first see value in your business. Since the value of software is in proportion to the size and engagement of users, it's a prerequisite for any company to reach the product/market fit stage before scaling. Product and market obviously go hand in hand. How can something be defined "product" without a market anyway?

This book will provide guidance, insights, perspective and inspiration to go from idea to product/market fit in three stages:

1. Genesis: the idea stage
2. Exodus: problem/solution stage
3. Numeri: product/market fit stage

Omar Mohout

Genesis: Idea Stage

In the beginning
there was the Idea

Section 1
The Startup Lifecycle

The Four Stages of the Startup Lifecycle

The Scope of
Master Class I

Idea Stage

It all starts with an idea. At this stage, all that matters is to understand in detail the problem or need that you want to tackle.

The main activity is gaining market insights through customer discovery.

Focus:
Frame the opportunity.

Problem/Solution Fit

Once the opportunity is framed, it's time to create the optimal solution and to get the first users or customers on board.

The main activity is solution validation through customer acquisition.

Focus:
Frame the solution.

Product/Market Fit

This is the magical point proving that you found a sticky market for your product or service.
You will also test your business model and pricing strategy.

The main activity is market validation through retention.

Focus:
Frame the market.

Scaling

Congratulations, you have found a market and a business model. Now it's time to move from being a startup to a scale-up.
You need resources for that: money and people.

The main activity is scaling by accelerating growth while increasing the organizational maturity.

Focus:
Frame the resources.

Moving Up the Value Chain

By moving from one stage to the other, the risks are reduced because assumptions are validated. The four stages form a value chain:

- No idea **creates value** until you embody it in a product or service.

- No product or service **captures value** until you embody it in a business model and pricing strategy.

- No business model becomes **sustainable** until you figure out distribution.

Getting business ideas is often not the problem, validating (value creation), monetizing (value capture) and scaling (value sustainability) is.

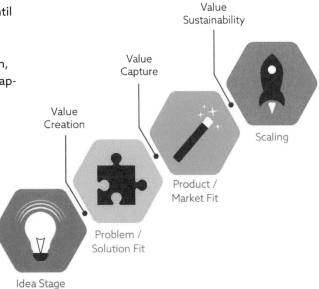

Value Sustainability

Value Capture

Value Creation

Scaling

Product / Market Fit

Problem / Solution Fit

Idea Stage

"It's not about ideas.
It's about making ideas happen."

— Scott Belsky, Founder of Behance

Section 2
The Truth about Ideas

Ideas Are Useless, Unless Acted On

An idea is not that big a deal. Millions of people get them every day. You can come up with business ideas any time.

We don't want to offend you, but rather help you adjust your expectations to the harsh reality of the business world.
A business idea is just that, an idea - until you do something with it.

A big idea is like betting all your money on a single number at the casino. It's a big bet, but you can win big too. It's a better strategy than a series of small bets, since the odds are structural in favour of the casino.

But entrepreneurship isn't a casino. It's both art and science. Focusing on a big idea may not be to your advantage. Instead you could come up with small ideas and combine them, as long as the end-result makes an impact.

No matter how great your idea is, if you can't execute it, you won't get their money. Luckily, the cost of getting business ideas out is getting lower and lower.

Expertise Is a Key Factor in Successful Startups

Startups have better prospects of succeeding if one of its cofounders is a domain expert.

If a founder with 20 years' experience in the insurance industry, knowing all the ins-and-outs, wants to shake up the insurance industry by starting up his own business, his chances of succeeding are good. He understands the nuances of the problem in that specific market, and has both credibility and connections. Compare it with a software engineer who wants to shake up that same insurance industry without any prior knowledge in that domain.
He has very little chance.

In an age in which technology is widespread and accessible, learning how to build a product is a lot easier than learning the intricacies of an industry.

Y Combinator graduate Leaky failed to shake up the car insurance industry due to lack of industry expertise, while Larry Page successfully built Google as a researcher focusing on the problem of scoring a web page based on links from other web pages.

It Isn't about the Idea

Investors increasingly show interest in the founders, not necessarily in the idea. They bet on the jockey, not on the horse. A good jockey can select a great horse, but even the best horse in the world can't choose its rider.

The educational background, a PhD in the relevant field or prior work experience qualifies you for the founder's job. Understanding a market without relying only on a big-five-style market-research study is key.

This deep connection between the founders and their ideas is called "Founder/Market Fit", where the founders personify the company. If you're not confident yourself that you're the best person to execute the idea, perhaps it's a sign that this particular idea isn't the right one for you.

It's like building something that you yourself need versus a cohort of MBAs fresh from university who are churning one idea after another, hoping that by throwing enough ideas against the wall, one of them will stick.

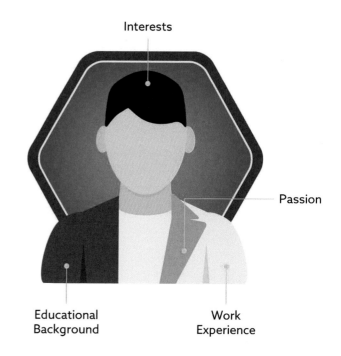

Interests

Passion

Educational Background

Work Experience

"The true entrepreneur is a doer, not a dreamer."

— Nolan Bushnell, Serial Entrepreneur

Section 3

Generating Business Ideas

Everything Starts with an Idea

People assume that an idea is a big aha! moment, but in reality ideas are just a "blip" in our brain. Most of us come up with small ideas pretty much every day. After all, they are just thoughts.

There are different ways to generate ideas. An entrepreneur sees opportunities wherever friction occurs. However, you cannot see them with your eyes, but with your mind.

Generating sound business ideas involves noticing pains and needs rather than thinking them up. Look especially in the areas in which you have expertise. If you worry that you're too late, that's a sign of a good idea with market potential.

In order to generate business ideas, you can either follow the What-Route (very broad) or the How-Route (start from something limited and go deep).

"An idea that is developed and put into action is more important than an idea that exists only as an idea."

– Buddha

Idea-Generation Techniques

1. Living in the Future

Imagine you lived in the future and began identifying what is currently missing.

Pay attention to early indicators of a changing context such as the arrival of electric cars, explosion of mobile technology, etc.

Live in a future 10 years from now, then reduce the horizon to 5 years as a reality check. This will turn your mind to the leading edge of one technology or another.

Source: Inspired by Paul Buchheit

2. Your (Previous) Job

Pay particular attention to things that bother you. Ask yourself "Why doesn't somebody make ABC to solve XYZ? " That's something I would buy immediately.

You can find great business ideas right where you work. That's what 50 % of the Inc. 500 Founders did.

Source: Amar Bhidé

3. Do the Opposite

Do the opposite of a successful idea. Think about Snapchat versus Instagram, exclusive (Quibb) versus inclusive (Quora).

Snapchat did the opposite of what successful photo-sharing Instagram did, by not relying on photographs that last. Instead Snapchat allows users to take pictures that disappear.

The Quibb platform did the opposite of Quora by creating an exclusive community—making it difficult for users to join—instead of an inclusive one, to which anyone can freely enter and contribute.

4. Successful Ideas

Draw your inspiration from a successful idea, but improve it significantly or execute it better. A lack of originality and authenticity should not be a turn-off.

However, just a small incremental improvement will not be sufficient. In the words of Guy Kawasaki: "Don't stop at doing something better, do that particular something 10 times better.
Jump to the next curve."

5. Use TRIZ*

TRIZ—The Theory of Inventive Problem -Solving—is a technology forecasting method based on analysing patterns of innovation. TRIZ assumes that problems and solutions are repeated across industries and sciences.

Investigating the technology patterns across industries combined with breakthroughs in science can result in new products and services. Breakthrough technologies determine which problems companies can solve.

More than 5 million patents were filed around the world last year, providing a wealth of information and insights.

6. Annual Reports

Annual reports of public companies contain tons of interesting and accurate information.

The reports show the risks and challenges a company faces; what's working and what's not. They also show a breakdown of budgets, so one can easily understand how money is spent; where companies are bleeding and; how their revenue is generated.

By comparing key ratios with companies in the same industry, you can quickly point out where everyone is suffering and where some companies are under- or over-performing.

* TRIZ is a Russian acronym for теория решения изобретательских задач or Teoriya Resheniya Izobretatelskikh Zadatch.

7. Apply a New Business Model to an Existing Idea

Startups are often obsessed with technology.
They feel as if innovation must involve inventing something new.
But an entrepreneur is someone who sees business models everywhere: they focus on ways to capture value instead of looking for technology to create value.

Don't underestimate business-model innovation, in fact more than 50 % of innovation comes from business-model innovation.

Source: Science, Technologie et Industrie: Perspectives de l'OCDE, 2008

8. The "Fractional Horsepower" Theory

The "Fractional Horsepower" approach is to take a single feature of a big successful platform and turn it into a separate product.

Think of Instagram taking the photo feature from Facebook, or Flickr starting as a game and then pivoting, based on one popular feature: image hosting.

9. Analyse Regulatory Constraints

Sometimes regulations are created to protect the market position of incumbents. In highly-regulated industries, you can find monopolies that are ripe for disruption.

Textbook examples are Uber and AirBnB. Think also Apple Watch, Square and Angel List as disrupters. Same goes for the health industry. Drones and self-driving cars are for the time being in a regulatory grey area.

10. Play with New Gadgets

Innovation takes place at the edges, just like the melting of snow. Often new technologies look initially like toys, unable to fulfil the "serious" needs of customers and users. But the underlying technology improves exponentially faster than users' needs increase. It's as if time in the technology industry moves in dog years—7 times faster—outpacing all other industries.

Harvard professor Clayton Christensen gives many examples in his book "The Innovator's Dilemma"; such as how telecoms companies viewed newcomer Skype as a "toy". Other examples of "toys" that became mature technology include drones, apps, crypto currency and 3D printers.

11. Go and Network: The Collision Theory

Network, not for customer acquisition, but for ideas. Be open and inquisitive. Find out where people hang out in the domain or industry you want to tackle. Get close to companies targeting your market, but also seek out differences and new perspectives. Gather across boundaries and disciplines to meet people who can challenge your world-view and teach you something new. It's there that you can expose yourself to fresh ideas.

All this can take place both offline and online. You might even bump into the person who will become your future cofounder.

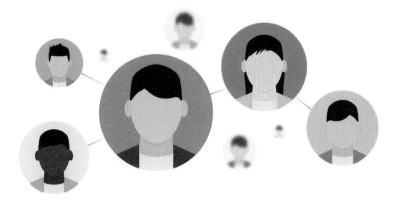

12. The Pain of the Pain

Any solution comes with a new—smaller—pain. The current solution of the customer might be "just good enough" or works only in combination with a semi-manual workaround.

Imagine selling new software for corporate training programs. If you would call them Training Managers, the first thing they will answer is that they already have training software in place. At this point, you need to dive deeper into the subject, finding "new pains" that come with their current solution.

You'll be surprised how many times the "business owner" is frustrated with the use or non-use of certain solutions they implemented. Helping them maximise their current investment is worth investigating further.

13. Gather and Brainstorm Ideas

Begin with lots of different ideas and end up discarding most of them. Use Occam's Razor to select the one idea with the fewest assumptions, and make sure you stay in one domain. Keep only one idea to turn it into a great business. Throw everything in it.

That's how Glow, a fertility app, came into being. Max Levchin, member of the PayPal mafia, and his team were brainstorming about the health industry, looking for underinsured areas that were important yet not life-threatening. Idea after idea passed until they had their aha! moment and decided to go with fertility.

Your Idea Doesn't Have to Be Unique

Valuable diamonds are the result of various cutting techniques employed by experts. Similar to diamonds, business ideas rely on execution in order to become great.

Coming up with business ideas is easy. Relatively speaking that is, compared with setting up a business and keeping it sustainable.

Ideas are often not unique, exceptional or great: - it's the way they're executed that makes them great.

Finding a great business idea is hard. A great idea doesn't necessarily mean doing something entirely new. Sometimes it's just about executing better or faster. An idea that is original but not great is not worth much. An idea that is not original but great is usually the most valuable of all.

It Isn't about Inventions, It's about Innovation

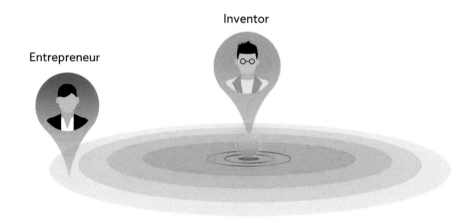

Inventor

Entrepreneur

From an entrepreneur's point of view, innovation is the application of new inventions to marketable products or services.

Apple was not the first to create an MP3 player, nor the first to launch a platform that made songs available to their customers. What made Apple innovative is the way they combined all the ingredients into a single music ecosystem while creating a great user experience.

As Tom Grasty said : "If invention is a pebble tossed in the pond, innovation is the rippling effect that pebble causes. Someone has to toss the pebble. That's the inventor. Someone has to recognise the ripple will eventually become a wave. That's the entrepreneur."

"The way to get startup ideas is not to try to think of startup ideas."

— Paul Graham, Programmer and Venture Capitalist

Section 4

Assessing the Business Potential of Ideas

Assessing the Market Potential of an Idea Is Impossible

You can't make any statement about market potential, because you're not the market. Actually nobody can, since nobody is the market (in line with Gödel's second incompleteness theorem).

The market for innovative products and services is simply unpredictable. No one knows how big the market is except the market itself. The only way to figure it out is by entering the market and collecting real numbers and real prospects.

Often, for new products and services, the market needs to be created and doesn't already exist. Remember, ideas are simply suppositions.

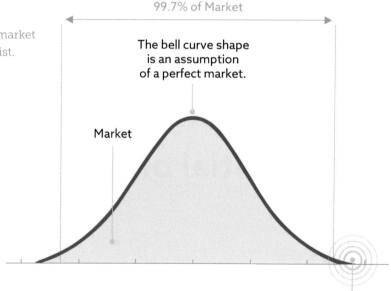

99.7% of Market

The bell curve shape is an assumption of a perfect market.

Market

You are here:
Gaussian
Outlier

Analysing the Book Market

Consider a publisher who reads a manuscript from an aspiring author. The "product" is already finished. What the publisher needs to assess is its market potential. Whether the publisher personally likes the book or not is irrelevant: it's about how high the number of readers will be.

The publisher has two ways, other than gut feeling, to assess its potential:

- The author has already been successful with previous titles. But that's not bullet-proof evidence for success of the next title.

- Take on a hot trend—chick-lit, cookery or fantasy novels— and publish a "me-too" book that surfs that temporary wave of popularity.

Other than that, the publisher has very few ways of gauging the market, even if he can estimate the "literary quality" of it.

A well-written book is not a prior indicator of success, in the same way a great idea is not a guarantee for startup success.

Dealing with Rejection on Your Way to Success

In fact, guess what successful authors have in common? They all got rejected. Numerous times.

- Agatha Christie got rejected; Dr Seuss was "too different from other juveniles on the market to warrant its selling".

- J.K. Rowling's Harry Potter was rejected 12 times before it became the fastest-selling book ever.

- The Tale of Peter Rabbit by Beatrix Potter was rejected so many times she decided to self-publish 250 copies.
  It has now sold 45 million.

- Margaret Mitchell gets 38 rejections from publishers before finding one to publish her novel 'Gone With The Wind'.

- Despite 14 consecutive agency rejections Stephenie Meyer's 'Twilight' goes on to sell 17 million copies and spends 91 weeks on the New York Times best-seller list.

- "Too radical of a departure from traditional juvenile literature."
  L. Frank Baum persists and 'The Wonderful Wizard Of Oz' sells 15 million.

We see the same pattern in movies. And we see it in business. Starbucks founder Howard Schultz was rejected 200 times by investors before he found the money to start the coffee chain. The rest is history. We can never estimate the market as we are not the market. Especially not experts.

Find a Problem Worth Solving

Startups tend to follow the typical technology-push approach, i.e. a solution looking for a problem. Founders pick a problem they think they can solve, rather than a problem that's worth solving. Yet it's easier to create a hammer when you need one than having a hammer searching for nails. People who seek problems outperform the people who seek solutions*.

One famous example of a solution-looking-for-a-problem company is Segway. The product-development cost was $ 100 million and it was touted as the revolutionary transport solution of the 21st century. But the problem they were trying to solve had alternatives: walking and cycling. It took a decade before they finally found a niche: security and law enforcement.

There is a strong correlation between your ability to find and frame a problem and your long-term success.

Solution

Problem

60 min.

"If I had an hour to save the world, I would spend 59 minutes defining the problem and 1 minute finding solutions."

– Albert Einstein

* Source: Jacob Getzels and Mihaly Csikszentmihalyi

Using the Market Matrix: The Shark-Bite Problem

The viable-business-sizable-market matrix is a simple and highly effective method of assessing the business potential of ideas using two axes.

On the Pain Axis, you measure how deep the pain is.
A "Shark-Bite Problem" has a big impact. If a shark bites off your arm, not only are you in extreme pain, but you bleed to death. However a shark bite doesn't occur often. If you find customers with a shark-bite problem, they'll be happy to pay you a lot of money to solve their pain. Unfortunately, not many customers have this issue.

In other words: you've found a business but not a sizable market.

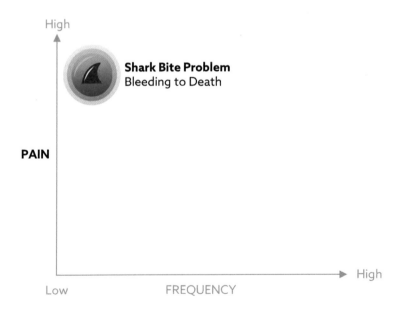

High

Shark Bite Problem
Bleeding to Death

PAIN

Low   FREQUENCY   High

Using the Market Matrix:
The Mosquito-Bite Problem

On the Frequency Axis, you measure how often a problem occurs. A "Mosquito-Bite Problem" occurs often but has little impact. Despite the fact that mosquitos can be annoying and you have to scratch the itches in the morning, it's a problem you can live with. The mosquito-bite problem is widespread, but the pain is so small that doing nothing is a viable alternative.

In other words: you've found a sizable market but not a viable business.

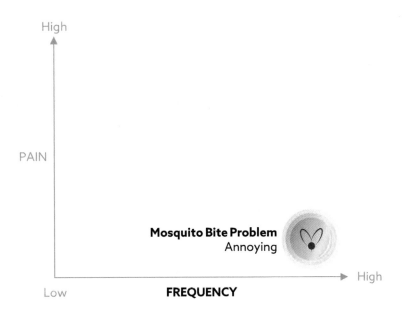

A Shark-Bite Problem on a Mosquito Scale

Business but no Market

PRICE

$10,000

$1,000

$100

$10

5   50   300   500

NUMBER OF CUSTOMERS

Market but no Business

Solving a shark-bite problem for a single person is called consultancy. However in order to build a scalable startup, you need to discover a deep need within a sizable market. A big and frequent pain can consequently be tied to a big and frequent budget (what is called Return on Investment).

The "Shark-Bite Problem on a Mosquito Scale" framework can be expressed as a demand curve in economics. The greater the pain, the more money customers are willing to pay. The smaller the pain, the lower the price. It's possible to make a little money from a lot of people, or a lot of money from few people. However, the latter doesn't add up.

The Recipe for Success:
Deep Pain and High Frequency

When you interview customers, ask them to rank their pain according to the intensity and frequency of the pain.

What you're looking for is a "Homer Simpson" or a "Cookie Monster" problem. Their minds are always focused on getting beer and cookies, as the needs are both insatiable (High Frequency) and instant (Deep Pain).

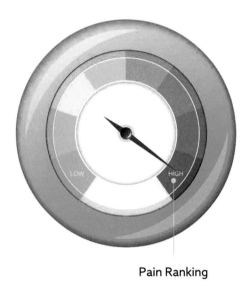

Pain Ranking

The Signs of a Mosquito-Bite Problem

Doing nothing is
a viable option.

There is no ownership
of the problem.

The inertia of the status quo
is preferred above actively
looking for a solution.

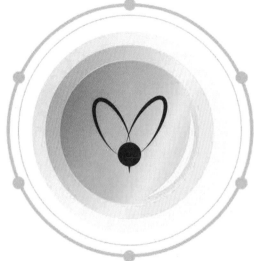

It's hard to get meetings with
clients to discuss the problem.

Microsoft Excel is often
used as an alternative.

Customer classify a solution
as a "nice to have".

The Signs of a Shark-Bite Problem

Customers actively try
to solve the problem.

You're worried that you are
too late to enter this market.

Customers want to pay
for a solution. Money is
the strongest validation.

Customers are interested
in the next steps.

Customers ask a lot of
questions.

Customers give you all the
attention and focus.

"Restlessness and discontent
are the first necessities of progress."

— Thomas A. Edison, Inventor and Businessman

Section 5
Changing Context

Look Out for Changing Contexts when Thinking of Business Ideas

A frequent problem with a big pain is that more likely it has already been solved by another company until a new context emerges, thereby creating a window of opportunity.

Take Google as an example. The invention of World Wide Web solved a need that had existed in the past, such as sharing and storing information and remote access across networks. However, a new context arose due to the large amount of stored information. This opened a window of opportunity for the minds behind Google to create a search engine that could facilitate access to the ever-growing online data.

If you're looking for a changing context and new trends, observation is the key skill required. It's where opportunity and preparation meet. Investors, bloggers, journalists and market analysts in a particular industry represent a great way to understand and learn about the markets they cover. They have both a broad, in-depth view of the market and trends.

Combining market information with technology-changing-forces is where innovation often occurs.

"But the truth is, it's not the idea, it's never the idea, it's always what you do with it."

— Neil Gaiman, Writer

Section 6

Entering the Market

The Four Market-Entry Scenarios

Scenario 1:
An Existing Product or Service in an Existing Market

You offer higher performance, better quality or a lower price. Because the market is known and consequently the market knows the product, the risk is lower.

The key to success is figuring out the go-to-market.

Scenario 2:
A New Product or Service in an Existing Market

Typically, the idea is based on a business model innovation in this scenario. Often the businesses opt for a niche, targeting a profitable sector of the market.

The key to success is the differentiation position taken against incumbents.

Scenario 3:
A New Product or Service in a New Market

A new market is created when a product or service creates a large customer base that didn't previously exist. Note that it doesn't necessarily mean you're first in the market, but that you're entering at the right time (i.e. not too early).

The biggest risk is market adoption, the point at which your predecessors failed. Apple, for instance, is a master at choosing the right moment to launch a new product.

Scenario 4:

An Existing Product or Service in a New Market

It's about expanding or replicating a product or service in a new market. It might be either a geographical expansion or a new segment in a market.

The Samwer Brothers' first big success is an amazing example of how execution can be more important than the initial idea. Inspired by eBay, they launched Alando, a German-language auction website, in 1999. Within 100 days of launch, they had sold the site to eBay for $ 54 million. There were at least 20 other auction sites in the German market at the time, but the Samwer's focus on customer acquisition outstripped their rivals*.

* Source: Techcitymews.com

The Importance of Right Timing, Market and Industry

The right market is more important than the right industry.

Southwest Airlines entered the long-declining airline industry which was the "wrong industry", but the right market of commuting passengers between popular destinations. Same goes for Starbucks, as it launched a chain of coffee bars when the coffee industry was in decline.

On the other hand, Better Place was in the right industry—Clean Tech—but in the wrong market of converting middle-class families to a limited choice of battery-swapping electric cars. It went bankrupt despite raising almost $ 1 billion from investors.

The right timing is more important than the right market.

Getting the technology right, but the market-timing wrong, is still wrong. Mark Zuckerberg, Bill Gates and Larry Page may be great programmers and talented entrepreneurs, but it's the timing that enabled them to build companies that changed the industry. The right market is not necessarily where it is today - but where it will be in the next years and decades.

Launching too early is as fatal as launching too late. The time and cost required to deliver on a long-term vision can be more than the market is prepared to invest.
Ask Webvan.

"If starting a business were easy, then everyone would be doing it."

— Common Sense

Section 7

Business-To-Business vs. Business-To-Consumer

Businesses Have Pains, Consumers Have Needs

In a Business-to-Business (B2B) environment, it's appropriate to talk about a problem or a pain. In a Business-to-Consumer (B2C) environment it's all about needs.

For instance, Facebook is not solving a "problem" or a "pain", but it fulfils a human need to connect and share with other humans. It's very likely that when you discover a human need, it will be universal, i.e. applicable to pretty much everyone on this planet. Humans are humans wherever you go.

The presence of a pain tends to be more obvious in a business environment than a consumer market.
A business has hard objectives that can be measured, qualified and quantified. Solving a pain or reducing a friction will always translate into a line on the balance-sheet or budget (so is the price you charge for the solution).

A staggering 54% of Millennials feel that new technology brings them closer to their friends and family.
Source: Nielsen

Learning what Motivates People May Result in a Business Idea

In B2C, people have objectives too, but they tend to be soft compared with the hard objectives of businesses.

Social, spiritual, physical and emotional well-being is important to everybody, yet much more difficult to measure, and tends to have a long horizon before the impact is visible. But it doesn't make them less important - au contraire. We all have powerful motivators within us. Such as the desire for autonomy, mastery, purpose, progress and social interaction.

If you can find the key to triggering these motivators, you've almost found a potential business. The last thing you need to figure out is what it takes to make the market aware of the problem.

Solving a customer's pain or creating a market need are two different things. It's not relevant whether it's a business or a person: the first step is for them to recognise their pain or need. Failing to reach an important objective for both a company and a consumer is a great opportunity for any idea.

"I find out what the world needs.
Then I go ahead and try to invent it."

— Thomas A. Edison, Inventor and Businessman

Section 8

"Ridiculous" Business Ideas

Ideas Are Never Ridiculous

We saw in section 4 that nobody can pre-judge an idea. Let alone guessing that an idea will be used and loved by millions. Consequently no idea can be proven a priori to be ridiculous. To go a step further, trying to execute a proven idea —something that incumbents with far deeper pockets and experience already did—is ridiculous.

Competing in such a "red market" requires a superior product/service or superior execution.

Note that history shows markets are not dominated by the first entrant. A first-mover often needs to burn a lot of cash creating awareness, customer education and needs in the market. Especially in B2C. The next entrant can quickly follow the pioneer's trail, unless they have a secret sauce that is hard to replicate.

Successful Companies which Started with a Ridiculous Idea

Facebook entered the market when Myspace and Friendster were the dominant players.

Amazon began selling books online when readers had to pay the price plus the shipping fees using their credit card, at a time when Internet users were reluctant to buy online.

Google entered a market in which it had to compete with over 10 successful search engines, such as Yahoo and AltaVista. Google took no advertising, thus no stream of income from online advertising, compared with the competition.

PayPal's alternative to the money transfer was to use insecure e-mail addresses to transfer real money, while providing access to bank accounts and credit cards to a non-financial, unstable startup.

Twitter imposed a limit of 140 characters on messages, in a world flooded with e-mails, SMS and chat boxes. It was mocked by Google chairman Eric Schmidt, calling it a "poor man's e-mail".

Snapchat created a mobile photo-sharing app where photos last only a few seconds.

Wikipedia came up with an encyclopaedia—for which reliability is the key property—to which anyone can contribute.

Airbnb introduced the concept of renting out airbeds in one's house to people they don't know.

* Source: Quora.com

"The way to get started is to quit talking and begin doing."

— Walter Elias "Walt" Disney,
Business Magnate, Cartoonist, and Filmmaker

Section 9

Framing the Opportunity

Act like a Scientist

Successful entrepreneurs see opportunities everywhere. They have incredible observational powers and question everything. In a way, a startup is nothing other than a temporary Research & Development laboratory.

Intuit founder Scott Cook noticed that his wife was struggling each month to keep track of their finances and used the launch of the new Apple Lisa computer as an opportunity to come up with software that people could use to keep track of their financial records on their personal computers.
Within his first year, Cook conquered 50 % of the financial software market*.

Phil Fernandez, Jon Miller and David Morandi started Marketo, a global marketing software company, only after spending the first year interviewing marketing people to understand their pain. Once they understood and framed the problem, they started creating the software to tackle it.

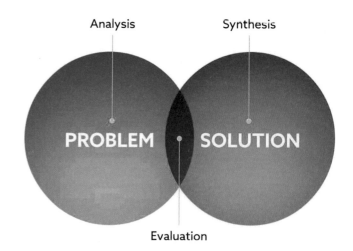

Make use of the Analysis-Synthesis-Evaluation approach.
Analysis is the process of breaking a complex topic into smaller parts to help gain a better understanding of the topic. During Evaluation, the information obtained will be assessed and judged. Lastly, Synthesis involves putting together the analysed parts in order to form a new proposition.

* Source: Dyer *et al.*, 2007

Act like a Market Researcher

Social networks can be used to identify sociological patterns and trends. Twitter is a good platform to see what keeps people busy by measuring the usage of hashtags, keywords, favourites and retweets. Twitter's Advanced Search even allows you to drill down to a specific place or language. Twitter is an open, asymmetrical platform, therefore it's easier to mine than Facebook, Google+ or LinkedIn.

You can use the Google AdWords simulator to gauge interest in certain keywords and Google Trends to see the interest over time. Quora and similar "Q&A" websites are a source of information to gauge what's keeping people awake at night.

You can also research the FAQs of potential competitors to find out what's lacking (i.e. integration or an unsupported service). Find out what their customers complain about. There are even competitors who publicly show what new features are being requested by their customers.
Such transparency is useful for research and discovery before doing customer interviews.

Act like an Anthropologist

Anthropology is the study of humans. An anthropologist is a master at observation while keeping biases, assumptions and prejudgments to a minimum. Clear your mind, just observe and engage. Try to understand the why and how, not just the what, where and when. Question everything, especially the parts you think you already fully understand. Listen actively and absorb what customers are saying, in their exact wording and language. Look for recurring themes and patterns.

Acting as an anthropologist will avoid the worst trap for would-be entrepreneurs: deep inside, they don't want their ideas to be invalidated. Any positive signal will be interpreted as a confirmation, while ignoring or avoiding all negative signs. It should be the other way around. This blind spot is the biggest risk you will face.

Pay attention to what Andres Glusman calls the "Malkovich Bias": the tendency to believe that everyone uses technology the same way you do.

Act like a Management Consultant

A management consultant starts an assignment by understanding the industry before engaging with a client.
They will interview stakeholders and study the document the client has provided. A consultant is using a methodology or framework to map out the perceived problem. There are a lot of methodologies and frameworks available which can help to structure your approach.
Some examples are the SWOT analysis, the Balanced Score Card, the Business Model Canvas, the BCG matrix, etc.

Be aware that what may look to you like a big opportunity may be seen as a big threat by others. Put yourself in your customers' shoes first, before you start talking to them.

Act like a Child

Nobody is more inquisitive than a child. Nobody questions more than a child; just ask any parent. Children constantly wonder about the world around them. They will question and question again. They will ask help and support. They will start playing with other children they've never met. They have all sort of dreams. They don't make any plans; they take things as they come. They have stamina, willpower and don't give up easily (like learning to ride a bicycle). And lastly, they are not afraid. They experience everything at first-hand. There's nothing that will ever replace experiencing things at first-hand.

Children are truly learning machines. Somehow we lost that ability by growing up.

Frame the Opportunity by Asking the Right Questions

Finding answers is easy when you ask the right questions. The right questions help you answer the different parts of the main question: "What do I wish I knew about my customers in order to frame the opportunity?"

Remember that you can't spot the opportunity from the outside, you need to get inside the building to understand a company's challenges and pains. And even better: get inside their head.

Explore broadly, but dig deeply in the relevant areas. Identify the key stakeholders in the value chain that are affected by the pain. A good interview will not only qualify the pain, but also qualify the reasons and measurements.

Learn more on what questions to ask at an interview on the next slide.

Sample Question Set for Conducting an Interview

1. What is causing you to have this issue?

2. When was the last time you faced this issue?

3. What went wrong?

4. What are the consequences?

5. How do you currently deal with this issue?

6. Does the issue impact certain departments or the whole organisation?

7. How are they impacted?

8. What tools and processes are impacted by this issue?

9. How common is this issue?

10. If you compare this issue with other challenges you have, how high would you rate it?

11. How is this problem impacting your objectives?

12. How much does this problem cost you?

Gather Qualitative Feedback

Although you're at the "Frame the Opportunity" stage at which you have the opportunity to talk to customers, it's a good strategy to ask them for initial feedback on your solution.

Try to find out if they:

1. Would be interested in your solution to an existing problem?

2. Would buy it?

3. Would buy it from you (i.e. a startup)?

Avoid generic questions such as "Do you think it's a good idea?". Don't ask for an opinion, ask about specifics. Generic questions don't lead to great insights.

Use interviews, not surveys. Surveys are valuable for asking questions that have a predefined or a limited set of answers.

During the customer discovery journey, surveys create more blind spots than new insights. Don't use surveys for discovery but for validation. Interviews allow for open-ended questions enabling you to drill down into relevant answers framing the opportunity.

So how many interviews should you conduct? It depends on the complexity of the problem or need, but anywhere between 10 (B2B) and 50 (B2C) is a good range.

Asking about Price during Interviews

Steve Blank is a promoter of gauging the price early on, even at the customer interview at the discovery phase.

Others such as Sean Ellis advise waiting before validating pricing until Product/Market fit is reached.

Our view is that, within a certain context, you can ask customers about pricing at interviews, but it requires a structured approach, not just asking for ballpark figures.
A powerful methodology for asking customers about pricing is the Price Sensitivity Meter by Dutch economist Peter van Westendorp.

Also check: leanpricing.co
Learn more on how startups should use a pricing framework.

The Price Sensitivity Meter can be used to measure the consumers' perception of the value of a product or service.

Interview Guiding Rules

- Begin by thanking the interviewee for taking the time to participate.

- Establish the purpose of the interview.

- Prepare opening and warm-up questions.

- Actively listen to their feedback.

- Ask questions, avoid making statements.

- Ask for stories.

- Any question that starts with "Show me how..." is a good question.

- A "budget due-diligence" approach will help you frame the biggest pains. The two key insights are: "Where does the money come from?" and "How can they make more money?"

- Assess the level of awareness.

- Remember that the user is not necessary the buyer.

- After every question, always confirm by parroting the answers.

- Alternate between opened and closed-ended questions.

- The more your idea is niche, the more research you need.

- Use silence.

- Pay attention to the interviewee's tone of voice and body-language.

- Show empathy.

- Avoid leading questions.

- Express appreciation at the end of the interview.

- Ask for permission to follow up.

- Ask for referrals.

- Create a persona based on this type of customer.

- Don't record the interview: people will not speak their mind on record.

- Doing the interview with two persons is a good idea (one guides the conversation, the other one takes notes), and makes you more credible. But more than two can be intimidating for the interviewee.

When you leave the interview, you should have a deep understanding of the company, the customer objectives, where and why they fail and how the impact of the problem can be measured in economic terms. After some interviews, you should spot a trend or common thread.

Cognitive Dissonance vs. Latent Problems

Understanding your customers' problems involves understanding their pain; it means how customers experience the problem, and why and how much it matters to them. The goal is to get potential customers to recognise the problem, and understand how they can solve it today.

When customers fail to reach their objectives, and actively look for a solution, it's called "cognitive dissonance" in psychology. Enforcing or amplifying cognitive dissonance is what sales and marketing people are good at.

However, when launching a new product or service, customers are generally unaware how it can positively impact their business or life. In such situations, customers don't have an explicit but a latent problem. By challenging the status quo in the area that you plan to address, the latent problem becomes a recognized problem.

Remember that you're looking for shark-bite problems on a mosquito-bite scale; a problem that is critical for companies and a must-have for consumers.

Using the Toyota Method to Find the Roots of a Problem

The Toyota Production System which Taiichi Ohno presents in his book covers the '5 Whys' as a method to establish the root cause of a problem. It borrows heavily from the laddering technique used by psychologists since the 1960s.

So, why 5 times? Each time you ask Why, it will move the problem up to a higher level of abstraction and a deeper level of understanding. It often leads to other potential root causes, and essentially reframes the problem. That's exactly why this method is useful when researching the opportunity.

The '5 Whys' will bring the problem behind a shallow technical issue down to a human responsibility somewhere along the line. Using this method, the owner of the problem can be identified, and therefore the persona of your future buyer.

Note that asking Why 5 times in a row could annoy the interviewee. This can be avoided by explaining that you use the Toyota method and by rephrasing the questions from "Why?" to "Show me how...?"; "How did this happen?"; "What exactly caused...?".

Asking the Whys exactly 5 times is not a law. It might be too many but other times too few. It's a conversation with the interviewee, not an interrogation. Once you've reached the boundaries of the problem you're trying to solve, it makes sense to stop questioning.

Because the Toyota method is a simple and systematic way to delve deep into the problem, it's very powerful, even for the first-time users.

Using the "Jobs-To-Be-Done" Approach to Frame the Opportunity

Another powerful yet simple way of framing opportunities is the "Jobs-To-Be-Done" approach of the famous HBS Professor Clayton Christensen.

He describes how a product or a service may benefit from using this method in order to solve a problem. Customers "hire" products and services to do "jobs" for them.
The method examines the customer's motivation by shifting from mere attributes to how they intend to use the product or service in order to solve their problem.

The concept is best described by fellow HBS Professor Theodore Levitt: "People don't want to buy a quarter-inch drill.
They want a quarter-inch hole!"

Clayton gave a great example in this video where he explains how a milkshake gets the job done. Click on the image above to watch the video.

People Don't Know What They Want

No quote is so misused in innovation circles than the famous quote from Henry Ford: "If I'd asked people what they wanted, they would have said faster horses". It assumes that people don't know what they want. Steve Jobs reaffirmed that thinking: "People don't know what they want until you show it to them".

But on a second look, the answer is there: FASTER. People want faster transportation, and that's exactly what the car industry gave us. There's a difference between understanding your customers by asking them what they want and doing exactly what they say.

The Idea Validation Process

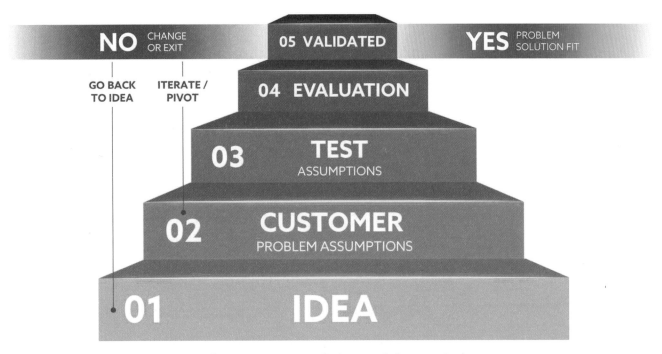

Positive reinforcements are easy to find, especially from people close to you. Try to find negative ones since they will help you to iterate or pivot. Successful entrepreneurs have a positive can-do attitude. They treat negative outcomes as a challenge to overcome rather than a reason to give up.

Applying the Business Model Canvas or the Lean Canvas ?

For startups, the Lean Canvas is better than the Business Model Canvas. The latter should be used by well-established companies. However, at the exploratory Idea Stage, there's no need to apply any canvas. After all, you're only trying to understand a single building-block:
The Problem.

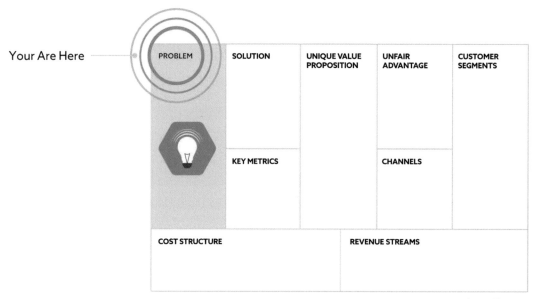

Lean Canvas
Source: Ash Maurya

"If you don't build your dream, someone will hire you to help build theirs."

— Tony Gaskins, Motivational Speaker and Author

Section 10
Protecting Your Idea

Share Freely, Share Often

No one wants to steal your startup idea. What are the chances someone will drop everything in order to implement your yet-to-be-proved idea? The risk that somebody will steal your idea is infinitely smaller than the likelihood that nobody will care about it. Even if everyone signs an NDA, what's to stop someone from making a better version once you launched it in public? So worry about the right things.

Share freely what you're working on as often as possible, and get feedback early. You never know whose feedback could help you make significant improvements. Go a step further and reach out to perceived competitors to find out why they weren't tackling the same problem. Competitors will often tell you who you should be talking to. The insights are more valuable than the risks.

Opportunities will materialise the moment you start sharing, helping you set a direction. You don't have to share your idea with the whole world, nor by telling everybody everything. You can talk about the problem you're trying to solve, but not how you plan to solve it.

Traction Attracts Competitors

Nobody will steal your idea until you get traction. Once you've proved that you found a shark-bite problem on a mosquito scale, be ready for tons of copycats crawling out of the woodwork.

The power of an idea comes from implementation. The prize doesn't go to the person who came up with the idea first, but to the person who moves from the Idea Stage all the way to the Scaling Stage while solving a Shark-Bite Problem on a Mosquito Scale. Navigating all these stages is not easy: fail and recover; iterate and pivot; adapt more often than a chameleon changes its colour.

Get customers first and postpone Intellectual Property protection until the latest possible moment when early signs of traction become visible.
Traction is the new Intellectual Property.

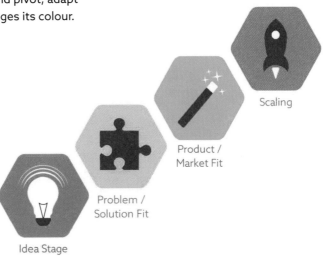

Idea Stage

Problem / Solution Fit

Product / Market Fit

Scaling

It's Not Patents that Protect Ideas, but the Markets

How do you prevent a competitor such as Linked-In or Salesforce from launching a new feature that replicates your idea? The answer lies in thinking about the opposite situation: how would you "steal" Facebook or Twitter? The source code for Facebook clones is freely out there for you to grab.

An application similar to Twitter can be built over a weekend. But that doesn't give you their hundreds of millions of users.

Facebook, Twitter, Google or WhatsApp aren't easy to copy because the value isn't just in the software platform, but in their user base. That's where the money is, not in their lines of code. Startups need to get traction in order to reach a tipping-point before the big boys wake up and attract the attention of the press, analysts and VCs.

Protecting ideas comes from 19th (Mechanical) and 20th century (Electrical) inventions, and doesn't apply to a world with free distribution and global market access.

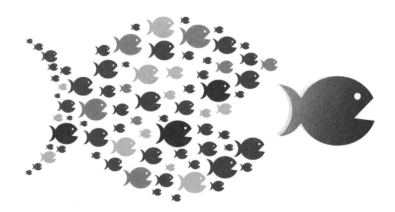

Sometimes in nature, the big animals eat the smaller ones,
but more often it's the fastest animals that eat the slower ones.
Don't be afraid to challenge the big players.

"One can steal ideas, but no one can steal execution or passion."

— Timothy Ferriss, Author, Entrepreneur and Angel Investor

Section 11
Guidelines and Further Reading

The Dos and Don'ts of Dealing with Business Ideas

DOs:

1. Frame the problem.

2. Focus on discovery as the key activity.

3. Aim for a profound understanding of the problem.

4. Solve a Shark-Bite Problem on a Mosquito Scale.

5. Bear in mind that success is 1 % inspiration and 99 % execution.

6. Share your ideas.

7. Connect with others.

8. Great ideas are nurtured, not born.

9. Make sure the interview delivers the data you expected.

10. Work to learn, not to earn.

DON'Ts:

1. Fall in love with your ideas and develop tunnel vision.

2. Avoid sharing or executing your ideas.

3. Solve a Shark-Bite Problem.

4. Solve a Mosquito-Bite Problem.

5. Assume anything about the problem/need.

6. Try to build a product for everyone.

7. Be an apprentice instead of a salesperson.

8. Talk too much, instead of listening more.

9. Avoid paralysis by (over-)analysis

10. Assume that others will perceive your idea the way you do.

Recommended Reading

Buying a $ 25 book is the best investment ever, as you get access to leading practice, years of experience and insights for only a "mosquito price". These three books are extremely helpful at the idea phase:

The Mom Test
Rob Fitzpatrick

This book teaches you how to conduct interviews and ask the right questions to customers in order to validate your idea.

Little Bets
Peter Sims

This book explains an experimental approach to assess the potential of ideas.

The Art of the Start
Guy Kawasaki

What does it take to turn your idea into action? Kawasaki uses humour to explain the process.

"Action is the foundational key to all success."

— Pablo Ruiz y Picasso, Painter, Ceramist, Poet and Playwright

Section 12
Conclusions

The Success of Your Startup Depends on Your Team's Expertise

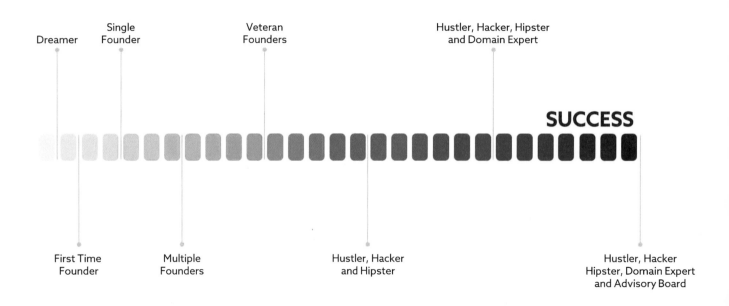

Dreamer

Single Founder

Veteran Founders

Hustler, Hacker, Hipster and Domain Expert

SUCCESS

First Time Founder

Multiple Founders

Hustler, Hacker and Hipster

Hustler, Hacker Hipster, Domain Expert and Advisory Board

Think Twice Before Starting Your Own Business

The step to launch a company should not be taken lightly and could be the most important decision of your life. A startup will take over your life to a degree you can't imagine for a long time to come, especially if you're successful. You'll be spending sleepless nights worrying or thinking about your business.

If you're a student, we strongly advise you to complete your studies first. Successful dropouts are the exception, not the norm.

As entrepreneurship is about taking tough decisions, you should begin with this one. Get comfortable with uncertainty: you'll face it every day. Startup life is not glamorous - most of the time nothing is happening. Startups have long periods of doing huge amounts of work with very little positive result. The emotion that you'll often feel is rejection. But decisions are temporary. Every decision you take lasts only until your next one.

By constantly doing new things, you'll discover your true vocation in life. Life's too short to pursue anything other than what you're most passionate about.

What Matters at the Idea Stage

Remember that what really matters is the problem, not the solution.

Keep in mind that while resources are limited, innovation and creativity are unlimited.

Frame the problem or need that you want to solve.

IDEA STAGE

Get passionate about the problem and transform that passion into a sustainable product or service.

Spend enough time with the people who encounter the problem or have that need. Seek to understand, not to be understood.

Assess if the problem or need is worth solving: Is it a Shark Bite Problem on a Mosquito Scale?

Brief Recap

Problem	Description
	A great idea that excites you and not your customers doesn't create enough value.
	A great idea that excites you and only a handful of customers lacks sufficient business potential.
Dream	A great idea that excites you and everybody else, but can't be implemented.

The biggest challenge at the idea stage is to frame the opportunity. Question everything and seek the answers; explore your idea from all possible angles and flesh it out. Indeed, customer insight is a competitive advantage.

The only metrics that matter are the depth of the pain or need (Shark-Bite Problem) and the frequency (Mosquito Scale). These two metrics are what makes the problem or need worth solving. A by-product of framing the opportunity is that you'll get an indication of the persona and the segment you will tackle with your solution in the near future.Once that's done, give it a little time to brew and take a deep breath before you go on to the next stage: Problem / Solution Fit.

Bonus Page

The main messages from the three most popular startup books summarised in one sentence:

Message	Author	Book
Get out of the building.	Steve Blank	The Four Steps to the Epiphany
Get out of the building with an MVP.	Eric Ries	The Lean Startup
Get out of the building with an MVP wrapped in a business model.	Ash Maurya	Running Lean

"It does not take much strength to do things, but it requires a great deal of strength to decide what to do."

— Elbert Green Hubbard, Writer, Publisher and Philosopher

Exodus:
Problem /
Solution Stage

Section 13

The Startup Lifecycle

Don't Burn the Midnight Oil at the Problem/Solution Fit Stage

Ideas don't create value until they're embedded in a product or service. Going from an idea to a product or service is the scope of this book part Exodus. This is the stage at which a company goes from 0 to 1 as Peter Thiel calls it.

Going from 0 to 1 is about growing a product.

Growing a product doesn't mean locking yourself away in a basement in order to create a product or service. As a startup, you don't want to create a product, you want to create a business. Interacting with customers is as important, if not more so, than creating a great product or service. This process of customer interaction is called "sales".

And sales matters as much as the product in creating a business, as it's almost never the technology that fails. So don't worry about engineering, worry about getting users and customers. Don't fall in love with the technology, fall in love with the customer instead. John Russell of Harley Davidson formulated this mindset as follows: "The more you engage with customers, the clearer things become, and the easier it is to determine what you should be doing."

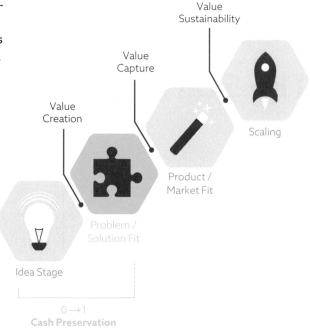

Value Creation

Value Capture

Value Sustainability

Scaling

Product / Market Fit

Problem / Solution Fit

Idea Stage

0 → 1
Cash Preservation

Customers Are the Ultimate Guides

Going from 1 to n is about growing a market.

Scaling is a concern for later, once you reach the "Product/Market fit" stage. Don't worry about building something scalable at this stage. It's the least of your concerns: just focus on building something people want. Market success comes from satisfied customers, not from amazing products. Ultimately, it will be the market that decides the value of your solution, and its judgment will be ruthless.

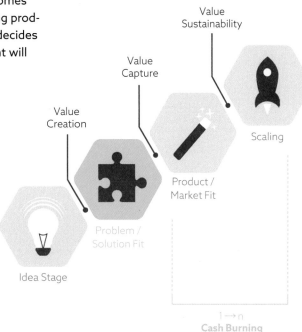

Value Sustainability

Value Capture

Value Creation

Scaling

Product / Market Fit

Problem / Solution Fit

Idea Stage

1 → n
Cash Burning

"The future can't be predicted but it can be invented."

— Dennis Gabor, Engineer and Physicist

Section 14
Problem / Solution Fit

This Is Where Your Journey Starts

Now you've framed the opportunity and know **Why** you can create value in this space, the next step is **How** to create value. If you want to solve the **How**, it's highly advisable to co-create products or services with your users and customers.

A product or service that fills a clearly-articulated niche and aims to delight your customers will go far in value creation. Connect with your early customers on the problem or need, and then— and only then—offer your solution as the remedy to that problem or need. Diagnose before you prescribe. There's a reason why there is a "D" in R&D: it's the role of development to make inventions useful.

If there are any overlooked assumptions about the necessity or purpose of the product or service, it's likely to fail, and no marketing budget will be able to save it.

The Problem/Solution stage is where the actual Journey of a Startup starts. Hence the name Exodus (Greek for "going out") of this chapter.

Turn Your Customers into Superheroes

Your product or service is simply about enabling people to do better. Formulate your mission as follows:

1. How to Address:	Problem / Need
2. Using:	Solution
3. Achieving:	Desired Outcome

Success at the Problem/Solution stage can be defined on two major dimensions:

- Learn how to solve the customer's problem and needs. You need to do their homework;

- Deliver on your promises.

People prefer to spend an amazing amount of time building the perfect product rather than getting a quick no.
It's not because you have a hammer that every problem is a nail. Value-creation takes place only when a customer need is satisfied.

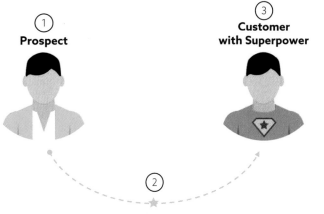

① **Prospect**

③ **Customer with Superpower**

② **Your Product / Service**

Increase Revenue

Decrease Costs

Reduce Risk

Save Time

Accelerate a Process

Improve Performance

Increase Quality

...

Make Them Happy

Early on everything is an idea, but once you have users on board you can finally start to find that nugget of value. Keep asking this question time after time: **What value will customers get from your offering?** Not features, not advantages, nor even benefits, but value.
Show persistence in finding the value: a "No" should actually mean "Why not?" for you.

Ultimately, from a customer's point of view, your solution is to solve his / her problem or need. If there is no pain, then there will be no change. You have to realise that not only is the customer buying the change they want, but they are also buying your ability to help them achieve that change. Even the price your customer is willing to pay is determined by their desire for change.

Startups are often proud of their ability to create great software. Just remember that the purpose of a startup is not to write code but to solve problems, and the best way to solve a problem is often to write as little code as possible. People don't care what you do or how much code you wrote, they care about what you can do for them.
First be useful, then necessary.

At Sherwin Williams, the word "innovation" never came up. But the word "customer" did—a lot. That has driven the painting company's success over the years. So make happy customers instead of customers happy.

Focus on Relationships

Asking the right questions will help you find the Problem / Solution fit:

- **Who** are you talking to?
- **What** do they need?
- **How** can you help?
- **Why** should they care?
- What is **unique** about your way of solving the problem?
- Why are you **better** than anyone else at solving this problem?

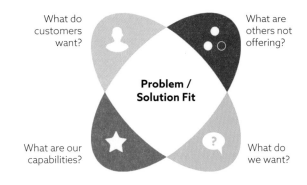

What do customers want?

What are others not offering?

Problem / Solution Fit

What are our capabilities?

What do we want?

Focus on relationships, not technologies.
Apply "agile development" when coding, the process of improving a product or service in incremental steps in response to what you're hearing from customers.
It fits with the lean startup approach*, which favours experimentation over planning.

*The concept of Lean traces its roots back to Lean Production in the 1990s, a method developed and coined by Toyota as it emphasizes a focus on reducing waste and continuous refinement. Lean came to technology startups via the agile community and was described in the "Lean Startup", the 2011 book by Eric Ries.

While the focus of Lean Production is on business value, the focus of the lean startup methodology is on customer value, and is aligned with the Customer Development methodology of Steve Blank.

The Lean Startup Cycle

The Lean Startup Cycle is a method to get a desired product in the customer's hands faster by accelerating learning.
The success is determined by the velocity (the speed of completion of a cycle), the number of iterations and finally by producing a product or service that customers really want. At the Problem / Solution stage, focus on qualitative not quantitative measurements.

Guessing what's going to work is a fool's game.

Value vs. Capabilities Matrix

Startups are defined by their capabilities to enable experiences and by the value they create for their users.
The next generation of those experiences will be fuelled by data, creating immense value for every individual.

Remember: Success is not a straight, linear seamless path. It's trial & error and keep trying. You should gain strength and confidence from each failure. The only real mistake you can make is the one you learn nothing from.

Increase the number of (API) integrations wherever possible. Find out how your customers work and add yourself into their regular workflow or daily chores.

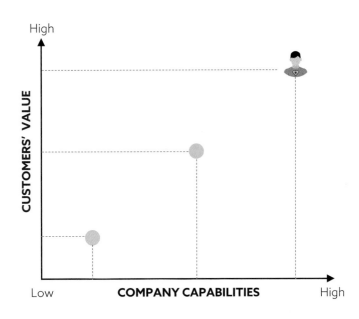

"Your future depends on many things, but mostly on you."

— Frank Tyger, Editorial Cartoonist and Columnist

Section 15

The Power of 10

Raise the Standard

"Best Practice" and "Best-in-class" are used to highlight what works best in a given established group. Being incrementally better than the class is enough to be "best-in-class". But a startup doesn't want to join the pack, they want to be an order of magnitude (i.e. about ten times different) better than the best. The best students are not sitting in class, they skip classes all together or drop out to create a class of their own. Following best-practice is a dead-end road for a startup.

Your solution should be 10x better than the alternative, not 10 %.

In the words of Andrew Grove (former Intel CEO), a 10x change is "a change in how some aspect of one's business is conducted becomes an order of magnitude larger than what that business is accustomed to".

Guy Kawasaki calls this jumping to the next curve, while Peter Thiel say: "As a good rule of thumb, proprietary technology needs to be at least 10 times better than its closest substitute in some important dimension to lead to a real advantage. Once you're 10x better, you can escape from the competition".

Ben Horowitz addressed this with "When you are talking about technology it means literally a much better way of doing things. To make money, it really has to be an order of magnitude better".

How Others Did It *

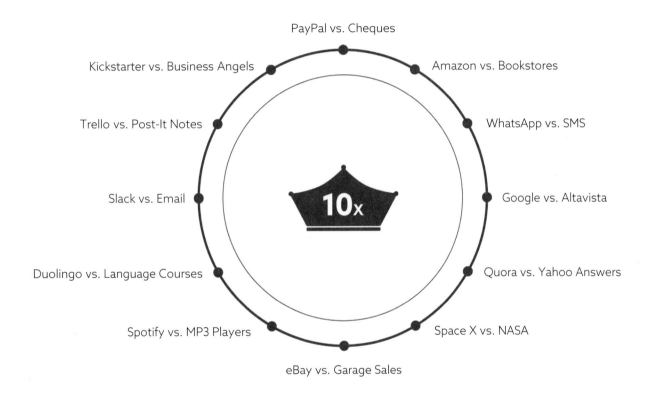

PayPal vs. Cheques

Amazon vs. Bookstores

Kickstarter vs. Business Angels

WhatsApp vs. SMS

Trello vs. Post-It Notes

Google vs. Altavista

Slack vs. Email

10x

Duolingo vs. Language Courses

Quora vs. Yahoo Answers

Spotify vs. MP3 Players

Space X vs. NASA

eBay vs. Garage Sales

*Products and services that are an order-of-magnitude better.

Why Innovative Solutions Fail

John T. Gourville, professor at Harvard Business School, did extensive research on why so many innovative products or services fail, despite the clear advantages they offer compared with what's currently on the market. He points out these factors to explain the frequent failures:

· Customers are unconvinced of the performance of a new product;

· Customers are unable to see the need for it;

· Customers are satisfied with their existing product;

· Customers are quick to view what they already own as the status quo.

Gourville calls it the '9x effect', i.e. a 9-to-1 mismatch between what startups think the market needs and what the market really wants. That translates into" You'd better offer a tenfold improvement over what's currently out there."

Overcoming Switching Costs

REASONS TO SWITCH

Existing Solution

Problems with Current Product

Attraction of New Product

New Solution

Switching Cost

Anxiety of Change

REASONS TO STAY

Switching costs are a major reason for pursuing order-of-magnitude improvements in costs, efficiency, and benefits to the customer. Switching costs are one of the most underestimated factors by startups, but are very well understood by customers.

That's why it's far easier to launch a new product or service than to switch customers away from a competitor's product, even if the latter is inferior to your offer. Old habits die hard. So when customers say your product or service is too expensive, they're not necessarily talking about your selling price.

The 10x Rule for Pricing

Let's assume a customer can increase his revenue by $ 10,000 thanks to a newly-implemented lead-generation solution. $ 10,000 extra revenue will translate roughly to a 10 % bottom line, i.e. $ 1,000. The cost of the lead-generation solution needs to be paid with a slice of that revenue, too.

Hence the 10 x rule for pricing: Startups leave 90 % of the created value to the customer while pocketing 10 %.

To move closer to 10 x value creation is to move closer to becoming a "must-have" rather than a "nice-to-have" product.

Check also: leanpricing.co

Assess the 10x Potential

Before starting to write code assess the 10x potential but make sure you don't oversell your superpowers.

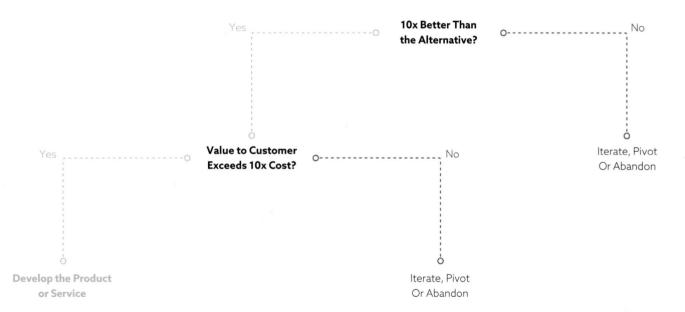

"For every disease, He has created a cure. So seek the cure."

— Hadith, Prophet Muhammad

Section 16

Who Is Your Customer?

Find the Right Market

Max Cameron said it best: "Start a business where you can easily get access to customers". In other words, select the right market. A market is a group of potential customers who share a similar need, pain or gain, regardless of gender, age, etc. that can be satisfied by your product or service.

Geographically-based segmentations are not good predictors of consumer behaviour and are often unhelpful in understanding target markets. A better method of segmentation is by taking the context and expectations into account. Using a persona will help tremendously in understanding the benefits sought, purchasing behaviour and usage patterns. Personas help to capture the drivers of behaviour, based on similar needs and profiles.

But that's only half the story. A market also requires a set of channels to access it so that there is efficient use of capital in reaching your customers. Understanding the customer ecosystem or value chain is of paramount importance.

By carefully selecting a market segment, it will enable you to build a better product or service without the constraint of the lowest common denominator. A market focus will also help you to develop a straightforward message to generate attention and interest quickly.

You will be able to determine the places where your customers go, their interests, and how they are spending their budgets.

It's Easier to Compete in a Narrow Market

A narrow market allows for better differentiation compared with more generic products, and it also allows easier referrals.

Y Combinator cofounder Paul Graham writes: "It's like keeping a fire contained at first to get it really hot before adding more logs."

Moreover, in a narrowly-defined market it will be easier to compete and dominate. According to Graham, it's a bad idea to begin with big ambitions, because the bigger they are, the longer they are going to take to achieve, and the farther you are projecting into the future, the more likely it is you're going to be wrong.

There is one caveat regarding a narrow market: make sure that it is big enough to support the vision you have for the company that you want to build.

Expanding from one narrow market into another one isn't easy because the market-specific value proposition is also a constraint. Adapting the value proposition is the obvious choice to enter another market segment, but that's easier said than done.

Startups that dominated a segment before expanding:

- Facebook (Harvard Students)

- Uber (City of San Francisco)

- Airbnb (Door to Door in New York)

- Instacart (Friends in San Francisco)

There is a rule in franchising that you need to make a store break even before opening the next one. Even Starbucks started with just one store in Seattle.

Why Early Adopters Matter

Within a given market, the most attractive customers are the early adopters. Early adopters will tell you their problem before you need to tell them. They're open-minded and willing to try new things.

Most people simply aren't interested in learning something new. An inferior product they know well will be chosen over any new and better one. Getting people to use and adopt innovative products and services is way more difficult than building a great product or raising money.

Startups naturally believe their own product is intuitive, logical and easy to use. This is called the Malkovich bias: the belief that everyone else is using technology the way you do.

For someone who never clicks on Google Ad-Words, it's hard to understand what others do. Actually so many people click on Google AdWords that Google became one of the most cash-rich companies in the world.

Getting people to try a new product is not nearly as hard as getting people to regularly adopt it. That's why it's called "early adopter" and not "early user". More often than not, people can't figure out how to use the product on initial use, and forget they even signed up. The early adopters who buy a Tesla or use Uber are not necessarily the same people who buy the new iPhone or book a holiday on Airbnb.

Being an early adopter is not a personality type.

Using Personas to Know Your Audience

A persona is a marketing concept that helps you to pretend it is the person to tell your story to.

The average user doesn't exist. Yet, it makes sense to create groups of people in your target audience who share similar characteristics. That's what is called a "persona".

Behind that persona are real people who you will be talking to at some point. It's highly advisable to use at least 3 different personas. For business-to-business products, create a separate persona for the various roles who are involved in buying your product or service. A company may have multiple buying personas. Typically they are:

- **Ambassador:** does the internal selling and has access to the decision-makers;

- **Sponsor:** has enough clout in the company, regardless of title, to push it through, even if there is no budget for it;

- **Financial sponsor:** authorising the budget and negotiating the deal.

In B2B, the return on investment (RoI), the depth of client relationship, the decision-making process, perceived risks and the industry context are all of paramount importance. Make sure you take them into consideration when creating personas.

Using a persona is also useful in creating different landing pages, at least one for each persona. Each landing page should speak to the persona answering one of their pain points, using language the persona understands.

Building a Persona in 4 Steps

Step 1 Answer the following questions:

PERSONA	NEED	WANT	BUY
Who am I serving?	What do they need?	What can I offer?	How can I reach them?
Example: Founder	Price Setting	Pricing Framework	Book on Amazon

Step 2 Create a fictional persona that represents your customer providing the details below:

- Name

- Education / Occupation

- Other relevant details

- Service attitude : Do-It-Yourself / Advice Seeker / Delegator
  Is your persona someone who figures everything out on his/her own?

148

Provide Context

Step 3 Describe your persona in the context of the (future) service. What are his or her objectives, both rational and emotional? Be sure to use characteristics that you indicated at Step 2.

- Who are they?
- Where are they?
- What do they need?
- Who are the people they follow and like the most?
- What do they read?
- What do they eat?
- How do they speak?
- What tools do they use?
- What are their problems?

Make a list with answers to the following questions:

 What can make your customer happy when using the service?

 What can deter your customer from using the service?

In-Depth Analysis

Step 4 360° view:

SOCIAL	OCCUPATIONAL	SPIRITUAL	PHYSICAL	EMOTIONAL	COGNITIVE
Relationships	Career	Peace	Habits	Needs	Education
Attitude	Ambition	Harmony	Physical Activities	Wants	Learning ability
Empathy	Satisfaction	Values	Disabilities	Desires	Reading ability
Interaction	Achievements	Purposes	Lifestyle	State of Mind	Open to ideas
Communities	Development	Wholeness	Gender	Feelings	Curiosity
Families	Financial	Commitment	Health	Sharing	Planning
Friends	Drive to Succeed		Stress	Stress	Tech
			Preferences	Self-awareness	Use of technology

Improve Your Chances of Success

Understanding a market and creating personas is something early-stage startups don't like doing. They want cool products, funding, website traffic, users and plenty of press coverage. Yet, all these are an effect, not a cause. Doing research, sales and customer development greatly improves the chances of success.

Market Insight

Success

Product / Service

"(...) Lightly child, lightly.
Learn to do everything lightly (...)."

— Aldous Huxley, Writer and Philosopher

Section 17
Changing Habits

The Key to Successful Adoption

The primary purpose of any product or service is to change habits.

All products and services are essentially asking their customers to do things in a certain way. The product dictates the behaviour and tries to make it a permanent change, i.e. a habit. That's quite a lot to ask. Michael Schrage from MIT calls it "The Ask". So it is a big task, but nonetheless one that can be accomplished.

The best measure of innovation is change in human behaviour. Stewart Butterfield, cofounder of Flickr and Slack describes it as follows: "Innovation is the sum of change across the whole system, not a thing that brings about a change in how people behave. No small innovation ever caused a large shift in how people spend their time, and no large one has ever failed to do so." This mechanism explains the stickiness and success of social media. French novelist Proust knew already that "It's easier to live without love than without habits".

Habits Can Be Changed

The best software is the software that changes user behaviour, so instead of improving your customers' lives, change them.

Asking customers to do something differently doesn't go far enough. Instead, enable them to become something different. Invest in their capabilities and competences to help them become a superhero. That's why Schrage believes innovation is an investment in your client, not just a transaction with him/her. If you can turn customers into superheroes, you'll also turn your company into a super company.

Habits can be changed if we understand how they work. Actually our life is simply a collection of habits. Charles Duhigg says in his book "Power of Habit" that, according to scientists, our brain is constantly looking for ways to save effort. So you need to manage customers' (behaviour), not products.

The litmus test for your product or service is simple: Would customers adopt it and, if so, how long will it take to turn them into superheroes?

* Source: NirAndFar.com

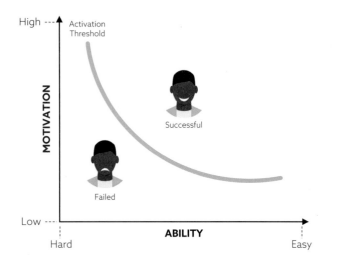

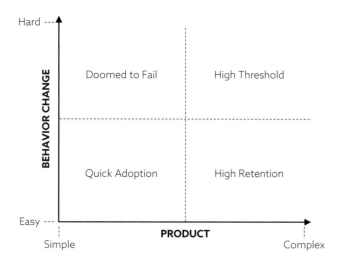

The Fogg Behaviour Model shows that three core elements must converge simultaneously for a behaviour to occur: **Motivation, Ability** and **Trigger**. Below the activation threshold it's the area where the trigger failed. Above the activation threshold it's the area where the trigger was successful.

By applying the Fogg Behaviour Model, we get the Customer Adoption Matrix.

The Hooked Mechanism

Nir Eyal is an entrepreneur and author who writes about the intersection of psychology, technology and entrepreneurship. His popular book "Hooked: How to Build Habit-Forming Products " explains how technology shapes user behaviour by creating new habits.

1. Trigger

The trigger is the actuator of a behaviour—the sparking-plug in the engine. Triggers come in two types: external and internal. Habit-forming technologies start by alerting users with external triggers like an e-mail, link on a website, or the app icon on a phone.

2. Action

After the trigger comes the intended action. Here, companies leverage two pulleys of human behaviour—motivation and ability. This phase of the Hook draws on the art and science of usability design to ensure that the user will act in the way the designer intends.

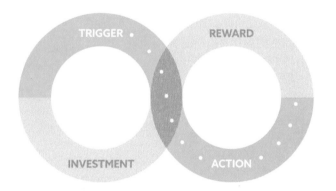

* Source: NirAndFar.com

3. Variable Reward

Variable reward schedules are one of the most powerful tools companies use to get users hooked. Research shows that dopamine levels surge when the brain expects a reward. Introducing variability multiplies the effect, creating a frenzied hunting state, activating the areas associated with wanting and desire. Although classic examples include slot machines and lotteries, variable rewards are prevalent in habit-forming technologies as well.

4. Investment

The last phase of the Hook is where the user is asked to do a bit of work. Investment implies an action that improves the service for the next go-around. Inviting friends, stating preferences, building virtual assets, and learning to use new features are all commitments that improve the service for the user. These investments can be leveraged to make the trigger more engaging, the action easier, and the reward more exciting with each pass through the Hook.

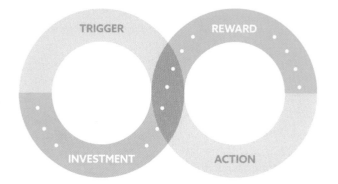

"What the world really needs is more love and less paperwork."

— Pearl Bailey, Actress and Singer

Section 18

Conducting Experiments

Learn through Experiments

Scientists do not treat ideas with kidgloves. They crash-test them. They run them into a brick wall at sixty miles an hour, and examine the pieces. If the idea is sound, the pieces will be that of the wall.

Experiments are perhaps the only way to reveal cause-effect relationships, as they can help you understand the (hidden) mechanisms acting behind the user behaviour we observe. Experiments can help us to set aside perception and bias, avoiding subjective opinions that can result in mistaken perceptions of reality.

They provide impartial analysis and information for fact-based decision-making on objective grounds, increasing control of the direction your startup or product is going in. Lastly, they help to identify the variables that play an important role and the inter-relationships among them, providing an objective comparison rather than subjective opinions.

The path to Product/Market fit is riddled with qualitative learning. Although it's impossible to set a deadline for Product/Market fit, well-designed experiments will help you to speed up the learning process.

The goal of Lean Startup methodology is to eliminate the high rate of non-adoption. Design your experiments with that aim in mind.

How to Conduct Experiments

Before conducting an experiment, make sure you:

- Choose a controlled environment;
- Make assumptions and hypotheses that you want to test;
- Test the riskiest assumptions first;
- Launch to learn;
- Manipulate iteratively the key characteristics;
- Investigate the impact of the resulting variations, as you don't know how you did it until you know how to do it again. But be modest in your claims. Statements should include words like "probably" or "likely";
- Learn the difference between a fact and a problem, as you cannot solve a fact.

Start with a small number of users, over 30 if possible—the more users, the more reliable the results—and make sure you subject them to the same conditions.

Or even better, just a few good customers is enough.Trust these handful of customers as co-developers, as they are the only co-developers you need. Remember that you want to test demand, not supply.

"Great works are performed
not by strength, but perseverance."

— Dr. Samuel Johnson, Writer

Section 19
Minimum Viable Product

Practice Makes Perfect

A pottery teacher split her class into two halves. To the first half she said, "You will spend the semester studying pottery, planning, designing, and creating your perfect pot. At the end of the semester, there will be a competition to see whose pot is the best". To the other half she said, "You will spend your semester making lots of pots. Your grade will be based on the number of completed pots you finish. At the end of the semester, you'll also have the opportunity to enter your best pot into a competition."

The first half of the class threw themselves into research, planning, and design. Then they set about creating their one, perfect pot for the competition.

The second half of the class immediately grabbed fistfuls of clay and started turning out pots. They made big ones, small ones, simple ones, intricate ones. Their muscles ached for weeks as they gained the strength needed to cast so many pots.

At the end of class, both halves were invited to enter their best pot into the competition. When the votes were counted, all the best pots came from the students who were tasked with quantity. The practice they gained made them significantly better potters than the planners in their quest for a single, perfect pot.

* Source: Quora

The Minimum Viable Product

The minimum viable product (MVP) is a term coined by Frank Robinson and popularised by Eric Ries.

An MVP can be defined as the lowest number of features needed to create value for the first customers, regardless whether they're paying for the service or not. It's the first shippable version of a product.

Ries offers this useful definition: "The MVP is the minimum set of features required to learn from earlyvangelists."
In that sense an MVP is your primary vehicle to experiment and learn in vito instead of vitro (i.e. to get your feet wet).

The MVP sets off the build-measure-learn cycle. You don't create an MVP because you're a startup, but because you want to determine the value for certain target groups. Launching an MVP means making your product available to some customers; and not with a press launch.

The MVP should be designed to learn what features customers are adopting (value creation) and are willing to pay for (value-capture). The results stem from many interactions between you and your customers, and between you and your team. It allows the most learning possible with the least amount of effort.

Minimum Effort, Maximum Value

An MVP isn't the fastest or a perfect product. Rather it's about minimum development effort that creates maximum value.

It is released to capture useful feedback on the differentiating features to ensure that subsequent releases will improve the prospects of success. Your goal should be to remove complexity from the initial user experience and message, in order to highlight the core value to the user.

An MVP is a path of very rapid iteration of customer requirements, followed by testing and validation. It will result in shorter product-development timescales and a faster path to revenue. In fact, this cycle, will never stop. You'll have to be constantly listening to your users and enhancing your product. To this end, expensive market research and subsequent product-development is eschewed.

Paul Graham rightly states that software is always 85 % done.
In other words, it's ready the day you release, but never finished. So be ready to treat your MVP as a hypothesis, not a definitive solution. Just like a straw man you are ready to burn down to avoid the Stockholm syndrome.
"If you're not embarrassed by your first product release, you've released too late," says LinkedIn cofounder Reid Hoffman.

An MVP also plays a vital role in designing complex systems as explained by Gall's law: "A complex system that works is invariably found to have evolved from a simple system that worked. A complex system designed from scratch never works and cannot be patched up to make it work. You have to start again with a working simple system." In essence, an argument in favour of under-specification.

How the MVP Approach Reduces Risk

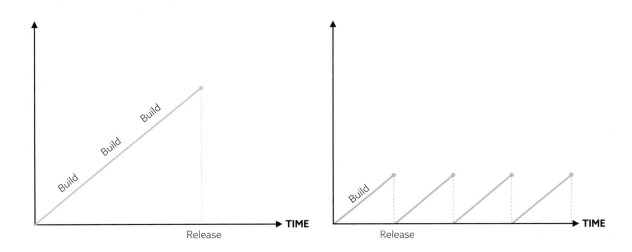

Do the least that gets you to the end instead of the most that gets you only to the beginning.

The open-source dictum, "release early and release often" has in fact morphed into an even more radical position, "the perpetual beta," in which the product is developed in the open, with new features slipstreamed in on a monthly, weekly, or even daily basis—Tim O'Reilly

Potential MVP Goals

Validate a product,
service or business model

Use as a demo
to secure funding

Demonstrate that you can
solve the problem/need

GOALS

Learn, rather than sell

Demonstrate that you can
provide the value customers seek

Validate a hypothesis

Demonstrate you're different

An MVP Isn't Always a Product

Successful entrepreneurs are not risk-seekers but rather risk-mitigators. The MVP will help you mitigate adoption, and therefore market risk.

Zappos started with one of the founders photographing shoes at a local retailer and then posting them online.
For each order he had to return to the retailer to buy the shoes and walk to the post office for shipping. Once he validated that customers do buy shoes online the uncertainty, and therefore risk, was eliminated. Dogs will eat dog food.

It also demonstrates that an MVP doesn't need to be a product. It's a common mistake made particularly by technical founders, who often think in terms of a final product and then start cutting features.
"Kill" developers, they are so time-consuming at this stage.

An MVP may be a landing page, wireframe, an advertisement or brochure, a HTML prototype, a paper version, crowdfunding or a clickable PDF mocking the desired flow. There are a number of techniques that can be used: just google MVP in combination with "Wizard of Oz", "Flintstoning", "Manualating", "Smoke Test" or "Concierge method". First see if manually your product works. Then think about providing it as a service before marketing it.

When building an MVP, the hard question to answer is how far down a particular road should you go to validate your vision.

Striking the Right Balance

The art of building an MVP boils down to finding the right balance between minimum and viable.

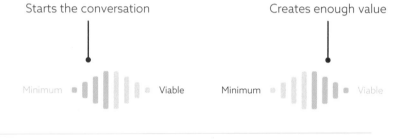

Starts the conversation

Minimum — Viable

Creates enough value

Minimum — Viable

Captures value

Minimum — Viable

If the MVP fulfils the "minimum" requirement but it's not viable, you're building products that nobody wants.

If the MVP fulfils the "viable" requirement and not the minimum, you're overbuilding a product without knowing if there is a market for it.

If the MVP is well balanced, a startup can quickly capture value.

Capturing value can be monetary, but more importantly at the Problem / Solution stage, it's about learning how to increase value and consequently value-capturing.

The Starting Point

An MVP should satisfy the following criteria:

1. Develop for the few, not for the many—i.e. for a particular type of customer;

2. The initial set of features should be rather low i.e. the smallest possible solution, but still representing the vision;

3. The customer gets value that is an order of magnitude better than the viable alternative;

4. The customer gets enough value from the product to make an initial purchase;

5. Achieve sufficient customer interaction to start the customer feedback loop;

6. Lightning-fast. If it's fast and ugly, they will use it and curse you; if it's slow, they will not use it;

7. Never force users to register, unless you need to do it to improve the experience;

8. Make it easy for them to learn how to use your product, as this is often the first major source of friction;

9. There is a failure criterion—what determines the failure of the experiment?

The MVP Litmus Test

You're not ready to ship unless you're ready to prove to your users that it's worth their time and effort. Getting the product out as fast as possible is not really the main point.

Keep sight of the direction you want to go, the vision, otherwise you'll not know what to test, and why.

- Test the MVP internally and with a few customers;

- Customers don't expect a perfect product, but they do expect that you listen and care. So show them you care;

- In addition to results, an MVP offers an opportunity to talk to customers. Discussing the MVP with users tends to bring up questions that would never occur to you. It's the primary source of discovering the Fonzie effect: a secondary feature becomes the core of the product, dwarfing main functionality. That's how Flickr came into being;

- Don't compete on features, compete on user experience;

- The outcome matters much more than the plan;

- Quick turnaround time on support queries should be a top priority. Scale the care by tearing down walls between development and support;

- Don't make customers happy. Make happy customers.

The Devil Is in the Detail

Don't waste time on small things. Inexperienced founders often argue what color a certain button should be, or whether "Try it Free" conversion rules over "Free Trial".
At the MVP stage, these decisions are often of little consequence and will play a role only once you scale. But at the scaling stage, you will have enough visitors or users to test things out.

Testing is superior to debating. You should never optimise before Product/Market Fit. Over time, everything can be improved. The Pareto principle states that 80 % of a system's use spans only 20 % of the features set.
It is not meant to be a precise measure of the ratio, but indicates the disparity between usage and engineering.
So work from large to small. Details often create disagreements, delays and meetings that cause friction within the team. That's why the product is a proxy for the level of collaboration in the team.

Don't be tempted to focus on every aspect in which your product isn't perfect, and don't let the urgent be the enemy of the important.

Paul Adams of Intercom gives his view on the tools used by a product team: "Using software to build software is often slower than using whiteboards and Post-it notes. We fight anything beyond a lightweight process, and use the lowest possible number of software tools needed to get the job done. If managing a product includes all of Google Docs, Trello, Github, Basecamp, Asana, Slack, Dropbox, and Confluence, then something is very wrong."

The Power of Sprints

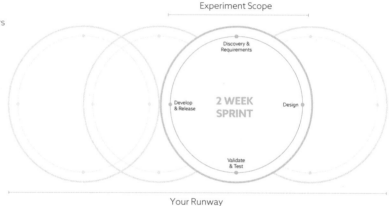

Deliver just what your customers need and eliminate anything they don't.

The number of sprints in a given timeframe is a proxy for your learning capabilities.

Experiment Scope

Discovery & Requirements

Develop & Release

2 WEEK SPRINT

Design

Validate & Test

Your Runway

In a group of developers, it's really dangerous not to set a deadline. The best way to launch on time and on budget is by keeping them fixed. The Saturday Night Live show doesn't go on air because it's ready; it airs because it's 11:30. As Fred Brooks observed "How does a project get to be a year behind schedule? One day at a time!".

So don't throw more time or money at a problem, but reduce the scope. There's always time to add those features on later. Work in 2-week sprints, but end each week with a demo. On Friday all gather round a big screen, grab a pizza and beer and let the developers demo what they've worked on that week, and set the plans for next week.

Focus on the User Experience

These days it's less an issue of creating a technology stack, and more about creating the experience layer on top of it. Building a seamless user experience is the most important factor. It's the interface that makes a product relevant and intuitive for people to use. As far as the user is concerned, the interface is the user. Making it simple and intuitive is no less than an art.

No　　　　　Yes

As Charles Mingus said: "Making the simple complicated is commonplace; making the complex simple, that's creativity. And the reason is simple too—to make the complicated simple requires a sound understanding of the matter and a laser-sharp mind to cut through the clutter and get to the essentials".

It's a good idea to start with the interface, screens and flow that people are going to use. If you get the interface right, it reduces the risk of getting the software wrong. However, it's not that you can focus on the various dimensions of a product in a sequential way. Instead of one-by-one, you need to provide an end-to-end experience, using a holistic view.

The Lean Approach Is Not the Only Way

Although the Lean Startup and MVP approach has been very successfully used by tons of startups, as with everything, it has its weaker sides. To take the Lean method as the one and only path to success is an oversimplification of a complex reality. Assuming that a linear and binary approach to finding a solution to a problem without any nuance is simply naïve.

For instance, focusing on fast cycles and iterations can pose a danger by giving false reassurance of progress and growth. It can also force the premature abandonment of an idea in the favour of a pivot. The other weak spot in the Lean framework is that it starts with a hypothesis—i.e. an a priori assumption that can be restrictive, leading to the so called local-maximum problem of Lean.

"MVPs kinda suck," says Rand Fishkin, a cofounder of Moz. Fishkin doesn't believe in releasing a lesser product, no matter what the benefit. Instead, startups should focus on EVPs: exceptionally viable products.

Also Peter Thiel has some harsh things to say about Lean in his book "Zero To One". He writes that lean is "code for unplanned" and equates Lean methodology to "making small changes to things that already exist." He argues that "would-be entrepreneurs are told that nothing can be known in advance" and questions the "make nothing more than a minimum viable product and iterate [their] way to success" mantra as the right way to go.

Pinterest is a company that didn't use the Lean Startup approach. It had dozens of versions of its signature grid layout which were fully coded and fully styled with production data before they were released. As its founder Silbermann said, "The hard part of that idea of minimum viable product, for me, is you don't know what 'minimum' is, and you don't know what 'viable' is.". As it took a very long time before Pinterest had users that became active on a daily basis, Silbermann is grateful that he didn't read "The Lean Startup" book at the time, because it might have led him to give up or pivot too early.

Lean may or may not always be the most effective approach to building a product an business. Like all frameworks and models, there are situations in which Lean is the best framework, and other times when it isn't. It's certainly true that the Lean Startup & MVP approach can be very powerful, but don't take it as dogma. A bold world-changing vision can be hard to apply using the lean approach. Would it even be possible for Shakespeare to write a masterpiece such as Hamlet in a lean way?

Julia Haines covered the lean-controversy subject in an excellent article: The Ritual of Lean.

"Any product that needs
a manual to work is broken."

— Elon Musk, Inventor, Engineer and Entrepreneur

Section 20
Features

Give'em the Pickle

One of the more iconic phrases in customer service is "give 'em the pickle," drawn from a story by Bob Farrell regarding an unhappy customer who couldn't get extra pickles for his hamburger.

The customer actually wrote a letter detailing the frustration he felt in his inability to get said pickles. The phrase stuck thanks to the important lesson Bob learned that day—a little extra effort in service is often all it takes to make a great experience. The benefits of fulfilling small requests give truth to another popular bon mot: "the customer is (almost) always right."

But what about feedback and requests that go beyond personal interactions with your company, and deal directly with your product? Should you listen to customers then?
Do they understand their problem well enough to propose feasible solutions?

When it comes to a product's vision, many will tell you: customers are often poor judges of their own needs. You'll find yourself having to say "No" most of the time, and it's for a good reason—in respect of building the best solutions, the customer is mostly wrong.

* Source: Gregory Ciotti, www.helpscout.net

The Problem with Features

When listening to customer feedback, the temptation to respond to anything they ask is always looming. After all, who knows the problem better than the person who faces it every day?

But knowing the problem doesn't mean they have the answer to it too. Listening to customers might help you to shape the destination, but the pathway there is your prerogative. Which is fine, because it isn't the customer's job to innovate your product or service: you decide what comes next.

As Phil Libin, former CEO of Evernote noticed: "Customer feedback is great for telling you what you did wrong. It's terrible at telling you what you should do next."

On top of that, every feature seems awesome to the product-development team. If you add every single thing your customers request, no one would want to use your products any more. Too many features create a mental overload, turning your product into Inspector Gadget. In the words of chef Gordon Ramsey: "the more dishes, the lower the standard."

Think Twice Before Adding a Feature

So before you jump on a new feature, start by writing it out in crystal-clear language, and pay attention to how this new feature is related to your core value proposition and vision.

If a feature doesn't have a noticeable effect on acquiring or retaining customers, or it's a digression from the vision, there's no reason to add it.

Au contraire, new features add complexity and create an opportunity cost. As a product becomes more complex and feature-heavy, its performance will go down. Remember, speed in itself is a key feature for all web services and apps. Each time you say Yes to a feature, you're adopting a child. Parents know how much attention children need and how long they are stuck with them.

Another pitfall is to look at a successful competitor to copy all their features because they are "market-proven". But that same competitor might want to remove half those features because they aren't used by customers, and just add clutter and noise to their product.

Copying competitors' features could leave you being reactive, and even strengthen your competitor's position instead of developing a solution that's an order of magnitude better.

Customers Know the Problem, not the Solution

In an article by Art Turock, Shark-Tank member Mark Cuban contends that asking customers what they want doesn't improve a company's competitive position. Customers make comparisons with existing products and service.
They rarely offer insights for conceiving innovative solutions to compromises that everyone reluctantly tolerates.

There's an enormous gap between comparing what exists and inventing one-of-a-kind innovations.

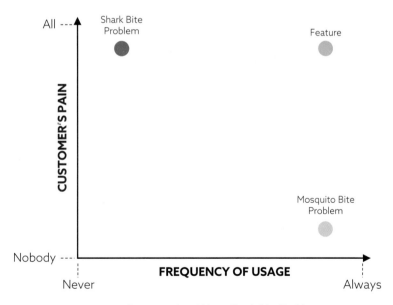

Features should be a Shark Bite Problem on a Mosquito Scale.

Questions to Consider

Before adding a feature, ask these questions:

- Is it a step further along the way to our vision?

- Will it matter in the next 2 years?

- Does it benefit all our customers?

- Will it improve the existing workflow?

- Can we scope it well?

- Will it generate new meaningful engagement?

- Will it accelerate growth?

- Do we have the bandwidth?

- Do we have the capabilities?

- Will it slow down performance?

The more features a product has,
the less likely it is to have what it needs.

How Will You Choose Your Product's Features?

Vision

Features that are based on the vision and an order of magnitude better than alternatives. These features are those that are distinct and distinguish you from your competitors.

Revenue

These are the features that "pay the bills" while moving a step closer to the vision. Cash-flow is the decision variable for prioritising those features.

Requests

These are features that are requested by customers, and are typically incremental enhancements. They are form the greatest threat of deviating from the vision - but completely ignoring them may alienate the customer.

There must be a hundred No's for every Yes.

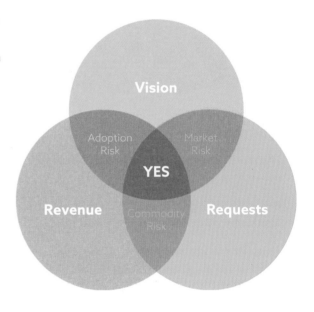

Feature Manifesto

- Our product should be feature-poor but experience-rich;

- Feature requests are considered the exception rather than the rule;

- The most expensive features are those our customers don't use;

- The more features a product has, the less likely it is to have what it needs;

- Everything that gets full attention will grow. That's why we consider one feature at the time;

- Features that don't add to the core value proposition or vision will be reconsidered in 2 years' time;

- Each feature will be described in writing using crystal-clear language before it is considered;

- We loath additional features as they are expensive, add complexity, consume bandwidth, increase technical debt, kill performance and require maintenance;

- All released features that can be removed without pissing customers off get removed;

- Every released feature should matter within the next 2 years;

- Any darn fool can make something complex: it takes a genius to make something simple;

- Each released feature must be demonstrated to all customers;

- Our most important feature is speed. Anything that makes the product slower will be removed;

- We build features which a small number of customers love rather than a large number of customers like;

- The most important button for every released feature is the "undo" button.

Learn to Say "No"

Saying "Yes" to a feature request from a customer is immediately rewarding. But you potentially barter a long term vision for instant satisfaction. Every promise of a feature is like a loan. You get the benefit today while shifting the cost to the future. And yet, saying "No" isn't always easy.

Companies that focus on customer success simply love to solve the problems for their customers and it's very rewarding to do that. People prefer to err on the side of generosity instead of caution in handling customer requests. Yet, your responsibility is not towards a single customer, irrelevant of how big they are, but to a market-vision.

It is tough to say "No" in the face of such demand, but remember that making yourself popular by saying "Yes" can only lead to a Frankenstein product.

And yet, saying "No" is not the worst thing in the world for a customer to hear. You need to communicate your vision so your customer is clear where you're going, what your strategy is and where the product fits into this. They don't expect your product to be perfect and they don't expect that all of their requests will be implemented.

However, customers do expect that you are listening and acknowledging that you care. Explain that you see how it might be useful and show appreciation for their contribution. "No" sounds better with understanding.

Always Keep Your Promises

So, the best way to handle such requests is to say "No" and immediately provide the reason. Explain what you're focusing on at this point.

Show empathy and an understanding of the request, but also be crystal-clear why you believe customers will benefit from the other priorities on the product roadmap.

In other words, give a good reason why the features you're currently working on will add value to your customer, while indicating that their request will be considered in the future. Avoid the word "soon", even when the suggestion is good and many customers ask for it.

The only thing you should never do is to say Yes and not keep your promise. Success at the Problem/Solution stage is delivering on your promises. Your vision and value proposition is no more than a promise at this stage.

So, you'd better keep your promises. As a bonus: learning how to say No isn't just a necessary skill for building your product, it's also an essential life skill. Buying short-term joy at the cost of long-term pain is a situation to be avoided.

"Direction is so much more important than speed.
Many are going nowhere fast."

— Unknown

Section 21

Design

It's No Longer about Coding

The last 10 years have seen an incredible change in how software has developed. Building software used to be like building a baroque cathedral. It was complex, needed a lot of planning and resources, and required years of development. Learning to write code was like learning Latin, it was hard and time-consuming.

Building software is now much simplified and the focus has shifted from producing lines of code to the design and user experience. Intuitiveness and the user experience of software has become a key skill to master in order to achieve success. Try to operate someone else's shower to appreciate how a very simple function can become a complex operation. Human–Computer interface expert Jef Raskin observed "As far as the customer is concerned, the interface is the product."

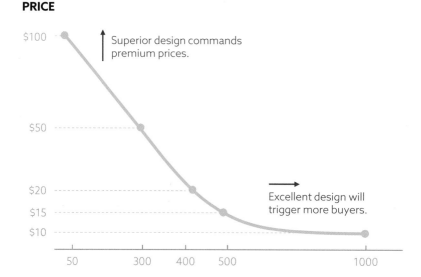

PRICE

$100

Superior design commands premium prices.

$50

$20

$15

$10

Excellent design will trigger more buyers.

50   300   400   500   1000

QUANTITY

Design Is Your Product's DNA

Especially for building an MVP, design with development in mind in order to avoid design decisions that will require further product-development later on. Too often, design is seen as an afterthought, a nice-to-have when development is complete and there's time left to look at the aesthetics. Adding a visual layer on top of software is not design. Design isn't the product's skin, it's the product's DNA. In essence, design is how your product behaves. Design is as importantas development. It's the second pillar of a product.

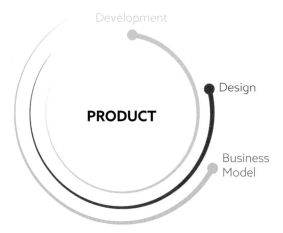

Getting It Right

Design thinking is the current hot thing which seems to be everywhere. It was popularised by design company IDEO and the Stanford School. It is based on observation (**the what**) to come to understanding (**the how**) and finally outside-in thinking (**the why**).

Design Thinking is heavily product-oriented and emphasises "doing" rather than "thinking". It encourages thinking as humans, not customers.

Design thinking is a broad term, open to wide interpretation. Therefore the concept seems fuzzy to people who are used to the clear process of creating code.

However, the benefit of using the method is that it's entirely user-centrically driven, as the user is most important. Focus on the user; everything else will follow.

Basically it's about "Getting the Right Design" rather than "Getting the Design Right".

Keep It Simple

The most important part of design is to truly understand your customers and users at a deeper level than even they themselves understand. In a world ruled by complexity, simplicity is your best friend. Simplicity means achieving maximum effect with minimum means. The designer's job is to give visual access to the complex and difficult.

Look at television remotes which have dozens of buttons, one for each function the remote does; a nightmare for users, and a dream for designers. Simplicity is often more difficult and will consume more time to achieve than building features on top of features. That's why Mark Twain said: "If I'd had more time, I would have written a shorter letter."

Design Impacts Behaviour

You might have a useful product with lots of attractive features, but none of them matter if the product is more difficult to use compared with the alternative. Design has a massive impact on behaviour, and good design is conducive to swift adoption. Make sure everything works for your users as simply and seamlessly as possible. However, remember the purpose of the MVP: to learn. Thinking that the product will turn out exactly as you designed it, is naïve. So experiment, observe and learn.

Just look at any popular product, you will notice how much effort has gone into the whole user experience. Those products can both engage beginners and attract experts.

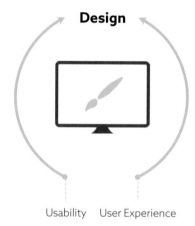

Design

Usability   User Experience

Eliminate the Question Marks

Steven Krug is a usability expert and author of the book 'Don't make me think', which focuses on the golden rule of usability, specifically, on the usability of websites, but the method can be applied to software products and services as well.

The usability of your product can be measured by whether your design makes a person think. The interface needs to be self-evident to both first-time users and tech-savvy users. Your grandmother would be a great candidate to test the first law of usability. If she is able to use it for its intended purpose without support, frustration or giving up, you can safely say you passed the usability test.

Usability doesn't consist only of the "design", but also the language used. If you can't make it obvious and self-evident, aim to be self-explanatory. Basically, it's about mastering the essential principle of eliminating question marks.

Eliminate the question marks and you'll increase usability. That doesn't mean you should patronise your users. Making them excited, creative, inspired and engaged, even if this involves thinking, is the ultimate goal.

Although the first law is the most important, Krug's book proclaims three laws:

- Don't make me think.

- It doesn't matter how many times I have to click, as long as each click is a mindless, unambiguous choice.

- Get rid of half the words on each page, then get rid of half of what 's left.

The System Usability Scale

The System Usability Scale (SUS) is a simple, ten-item questionnaire to assess usability, developed by John Brooke. Although it is subjective, it has been shown to be a reliable and valid instrument, even with a small number of participants.

	STRONGLY DISAGREE				STRONGLY AGREE
	1	2	3	4	5
1. I think that I would like to use this system frequently.					
2. I found the system unnecessarily complex.					
3. I thought the system was easy to use.					
4. I think that I would need the support of a technical person to be able to use this system.					
5. I found the various functions in this system were well integrated.					
6. I thought there was too much inconsistency in this system.					
7. I would imagine that most people would learn to use this system very quickly.					
8. I found the system very cumbersome to use.					
9. I felt very confident using the system.					
10. I needed to learn a lot of things before I could get going with this system.					

For the odd items, subtract one from the user response and for the even-numbered items, subtract the user responses from 5. This scales all values from 0 to 4. Add up the converted responses and multiply that total by 2.5 to convert to a scale from 0 to 100.

The Importance of Art

The design of a product or service is not the outcome of rational thinking, rather it's a work of art. Think of art as a way to connect technology and people to make an impact. After all, that's the ultimate purpose of art: to make an impact on people. To understand art is to understand human psychology, resulting in superior products.

There's also a difference between design and art. The former is about solving problems, whereas the latter is about asking questions. Design is there to fill a human or business need, whereas art exist for its own sake.

If you want to learn about the art of simplicity and usability, look at books intended for toddlers. They have the best UX Design: even tiny tots can understand it. Check out the iconic cartoon characters of Musti created by Belgian graphic artist Ray Goossens in 1969 and; Miffy, drawn and written by Dutch artist Dick Bruna in 1955 for inspiration.

"The life of a man who wants to fly consists mainly of falling."

— Arthur Japin, Novelist

Section 22
Business Model

Value Capture Rules Value Creation

Herbert Dow founded Dow Chemical in Midland, Michigan, when he invented a way to produce bromine cheaply.

He sold the chemical for industrial purposes all over the US for 36 cents a pound at the turn of the 20th century.

He couldn't go overseas, however, because the international market was controlled by a giant German chemical cartel which sold it at a fixed price of 49 cents a pound. It was understood that the Germans would stay out of the US market so long as Dow and the other American suppliers stayed within its borders.

Eventually Dow's business was in trouble and he had to expand. He took his bromine to England and easily beat the cartel's fixed price of 49 cents a pound. Things were okay for a while until a German visitor came to Michigan and threatened Dow that he had to cease and desist.

Dow didn't like being told what to do and told the cartel to get lost. Shortly thereafter German bromine started appearing for sale in the US for 15 cents a pound, way below Dow's price. The cartel flooded the US market, offering the chemical way below their own costs, intending to drive Dow out of business.

* Source: David Fry, Quora

But Dow outsmarted them. He stopped selling in the US market entirely and instead arranged for someone to secretly start buying up all the German bromine he could get his hands on. Dow repackaged it as his own product, shipped it to Europe, and made it widely available (even in Germany) at 27 cents a pound. The Germans were wondering why Dow wasn't out of business, and why there was suddenly such demand for bromine in the US?

The cartel lowered its price to 12 cents and then 10 cents. Dow just kept buying more and more, gaining huge market share in Europe. Finally the Germans caught on and had to lower their prices at home. Dow had broken the German chemical monopoly and expanded his business greatly. And customers got a wider range of places to buy bromine at lower prices. Dow went on to do the same trick to the German dye and magnesium monopolies. This is now the textbook way to deal with predatory price cutting.

* Source: David Fry, Quora

The Importance of a Business Model

The moment when a startup creates a product or service is the moment value is created. Even if only a single user is using it or the internal team, some value is created. However, it's perfectly possible that a startup creates a lot of value without itself becoming valuable.

For a company to be sustainable, it's equally—if not more— important to capture part of the value that has been created. Value must be created, delivered and accepted by customers before any of it becomes available for capture. Too often startups assume that if value is created, rewards will follow.

Just as an MVP needs to be viable, a startup also needs a viable business model as a basis for the venture's economic success. Often startups fail to capture value from new technology they created, because it's not embedded in an economically viable business model. The product itself is only one of the many components of a business model.

Airbnb and Uber's success relies more on business than on technology: their main innovation was to redefine the category of holiday renting and taxis. Never underestimate business-model innovation: Tupperware had a business model that was defensible and sustainable for 50 years.

The Business Model Impacts the Whole Company

At the Problem/Solution stage, the business model is more of a hypothesis, an initial exploratory experiment. Identifying and executing a business model is an entrepreneurial act which requires insight into both the technology and the market.

A business model is the true product of an entrepreneur. It's the way to create value for him/herself and the shareholders. That's why many VCs invest in business models, not in technology. By building a startup, you're in fact building a money-making machine.

If a business model is changed, consequently the go-to-market and support organisation needs to change as well. This is one of the reasons why it's such a challenge for existing companies to launch an innovative product or service. It might require a transformation of all levels of the organisation; even the company's DNA and culture needs to adapt.

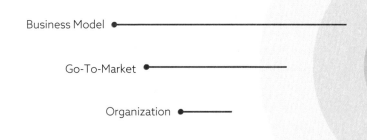

The different layers needed to support the product from a business and commercial point of view.

It's All about Survival

A a business model is essentially how an organisation sustains itself financially. To survive and thrive, organisations need to have a viable business model. At the beginning of a startup, the "viable" comes from the time and money of the cofounders, FFF and grants. But over time, it's likely that it will have to come from the paying customer.

That's why Peter Drucker describes a business model as "no more than a representation of how an organisation makes (or intends to make) money".

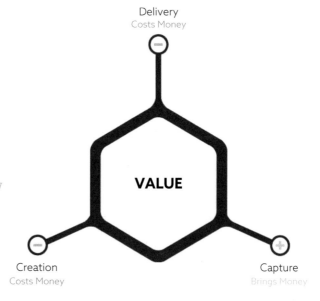

Delivery
Costs Money

VALUE

Creation
Costs Money

Capture
Brings Money

How to Capture Value

The first step toward value-capture is simply to make users and customers aware of it.

For instance, WhatsApp is free to download and try for the first year. After a year, you have the option of extending your subscription for $ 0.99 / year.
However, users are made aware the moment they sign up that in 1 year's time a fee will be charged, even as small as $ 0.99!

- -

There are **2 major ways** to capture value:

- The pricing strategy: getting paid by the customers for the product or service;

- The business model.

- -

To capture value without charging money, you need to identify customers who are unwilling or unable to pay, but have a need for a given product or service. Next, you have to determine how to capture value from these segments. An example of how the business model can capture value is Waze.

Waze is a community-based traffic and navigation app acquired by Google. Waze provides a lot of value to its users, but asks for the data back in return (such as speed, location, etc). It collects the data through licensing or through selling location-based advertising.

The Waze business model is interesting as it has a network effect by default. A network effect, or Metcalfe's law, means that each new user adds value to other users. Think about the first telephone. It had no value because there was no one else you could call. The more people who use telephones, the higher the value for everyone in the network. As only a rather low percentage of users will add value to your application, make sure to aggregate user data as a side-effect of their usage.

As they say: If you're not paying for it, you're not the customer; you're the product being sold. Ultimately someone has to pick up the bill.

The Business-Model Canvas or the Lean Canvas?

For startups, the Lean Canvas is superior to the Business-Model Canvas. The latter should be used by established companies, and is great for describing the current situation, but is not intended for startups. Filling the whole canvas at once for a new product in a new market is simply overkill, unless you have an existing significant business.

At the Problem/Solution Stage, there is no need to apply a canvas at all. The Lean Canvas will be covered in the next "Master-class: Product/Market Fit", because that's the stage at which all business model components need to be validated.

At the Problem/Solution stage, focus on making something people want, i.e. frame the solution, as that is the heart of the business model anyway.

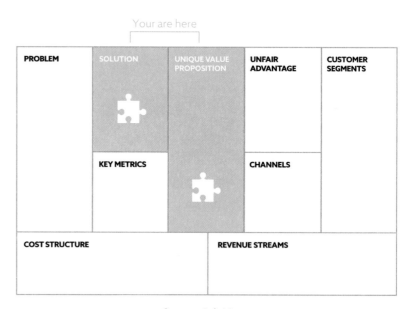

Source: Ash Maurya

Author Ash Maurya finds that too many founders carry their hypotheses in their heads alone, a strategy that does not provide an enriching feedback cycle to test and refine their ideas.

"It's a funny thing about life;
if you refuse to accept anything
but the best, you very often get it."

— Somerset Maugham,
Playwright, Novelist and Writer

Section 23

Value Proposition

What Is a Value Proposition?

The value proposition is a single clear, compelling and concise message that states why your product or service is different and worth buying.

A value proposition is important to all stakeholders and can be used as core for pitching customers, partners, VCs and new hires. Although it is part of it, don't confuse a value proposition with an elevator pitch. The value proposition is the value put on the social or economic benefit for which a customer will pay.

Try to summarise the value proposition in 30 words or less. Since the value proposition is the core of a business model, take the time to condense it into a brief statement. It should be long enough to cover the subject and short enough to keep it interesting. Words are the best fuel for great marketing, i.e., communicating the value to the market. So pick your words carefully and keep the target market in mind. A value proposition is not a description of your product or service. Rather it captures what you want to do, how you want to do it, and why it matters to your customer.

Make It Relevant to Your Customers

A value proposition is a clear statement of the tangible results a customer will get from your product or service.

It's the basic reason why a customer should consider your product or service. It should arouse interest and provide the key reasons that your customers buy from you rather than from someone else.

What distinguishes you from other vendors is called the unique selling proposition (USP). Given that a USP creates competitive differentiation, it works only for customers who are ready to buy. It's the value proposition that generates interest and desire in the target group.

Value proposition is about relevance, whereas a USP is about the uniqueness of your product or service.

- -

A value proposition typically has **three components**, which can be formulated as answers to these questions:

- **What** are you offering to customers?

- **How** does it benefit the customer?

- **To whom** you are offering it?

- -

Walk in Their Shoes

Dare to be different as long as your difference matters. Derive your value proposition from the problem or need you're solving. Use the world-view of the customers you're targeting to give context, and don't be afraid to be bold and specific to get inside your customer's head.

Put yourself in their shoes, use the personas you created, and try to understand what you're offering from their point of view. Just as it's your job to build a product that really does make people's working lives better; it's also your job to understand what people think they want and translate the value of your product into their own terms.

A well formulated value proposition matches your product or service with the problem or needs of a particular customer, while highlighting the difference with alternatives. In other words: how you help them and why you stand out.

The customer experience is the core of the value proposition.

Researching the Value Proposition

As you target a particular customer segment, hang out at forums, groups, blogs and social media in order to understand how they perceive and articulate their problem and needs. This is called a "value proposition safari".

Listen to how people talk about what they want to achieve. This is what Clayton Christensen calls "jobs be done".

- -

His colleague Ted Levitt gives some examples:

- People don't want a quarter-inch drill - they want a quarter-inch hole

- People don't need socks, they need their feet to be less cold

- Doctors want more patients, not an efficient scheduling tool

- -

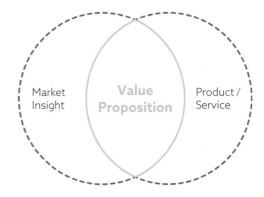

A well-executed value proposition safari will bring you new ways of articulating the value, and refinements to how to convey this value.

Test Your Value Proposition

Does it:

- Start from the customer's world-view?

- Encapsulate the value you offer?

- Capture what you do?

- Highlight the USPs?

- Articulate what can be achieved?

- State how it will be achieved?

- State why it matters?

- Use the language of the target group?

- Describe the "job be done"?

Is it:

- Easy to understand?

- Compelling and concise?

- Align with the company's DNA?

- Honest?

- Distinctive enough?

- Aligned with your vision?

- Long enough to cover the subject?

- Short enough to keep it interesting?

Slack's Value Proposition

The following memo was sent to the team at Slack by cofounder Stewart Butterfield:

We're unlikely to be able to sell "a group chat system" very well: there are just not enough people shopping for group chat systems. That's why what we're selling is organisational transformation. What we are selling is not the software product —the set of all the features, in their specific implementation— because there are just not many buyers for that software product. (People buy "software" to address a need they already know they have, or perform some specific task they need to perform, whether that is tracking sales contacts or editing video.)

However, if we're selling "a reduction in the cost of communication" or "zero effort knowledge management" or "making better decisions, faster" or "all your team communication, instantly searchable, available wherever you go" or "75 % less e-mail" or some other valuable result of adopting Slack, we will find many more buyers. That's why what we're selling is organisational transformation. The software just happens to be the part we're able to build & ship (and the means for us to get our cut).

We're selling a reduction in information overload, relief from stress, and a new ability to extract the enormous value of hitherto-useless corporate archives. We're selling better organisations, better teams. That's a good thing for people to buy, and it's a much better thing for us to sell in the long run. We will be successful to the extent that we create better teams.

* Source: We Don't Sell Saddles Here, Medium

Experience and Service Are the Ingredients for Success

Even the best-formulated value proposition will fall down if it's not supported by the experience people have when they start using the product. Take the case of GoPro: who needs another camera? Everyone has one, and the market for cameras is dominated by Japanese companies. But GoPro founder Nick Woodman was simply brilliant: he sold the experience, not the device itself. The camera is just a way to get the experience.

The route to a vibrant, thriving and growing business is often the service. That's why decisions that concern your business model depend heavily on your value proposition.

The value proposition should be credible and aligned with the DNA and identity of your company. It's not the "Brand" – it's the "Experience". Summing up features isn't the answer. Formulating both the pain and the solution is.

* Source: We Don't Sell Saddles Here, Medium

The IKEA Effect

Founders are totally in love with the technology they've created. This is called the IKEA effect. When you make something yourself, you value it way more than you should and therefore overvalue it. Be aware of the IKEA effect to avoid this bias.

What it all boils down to: can you genuinely help your customers overcome their obstacles and help them grow?
Your product or service is necessary to take them there, it's the framework that makes it possible but it's not what people care about. Put yourself in their shoes, empathise with them and start an honest dialogue.

Final advice: a value proposition is not set in stone and can evolve over time. It's an iterative process. Greatness doesn't come overnight.

"People don't care how much you know, until they know how much you care about them."

— John C. Maxwell, Author, Speaker and Pastor

Section 24

Guidelines and Further Reading

Guidelines for Founders

Great founders are listeners:

Not seeking or using customer feedback is the worst thing you can do. The very best founders are great listeners. As Bill Gates once famously said about customers "They may not tell you what you should build but they can surely tell what's wrong."

So seek to understand (the problem) before you seek to be understood (the solution).

Great founders care:

People don't care about what you do, they care about what you can do for them. Caring about your customers' success strengthens your connection to them. Customer appreciation is often viewed as a lost art.

The art of genuinely caring about the customer is the key to winning people over for life.

Great founders understand behaviour:

Your real competition is not who you think they are, but who your customers think they are. What is worse than not having an MVP? Having one that nobody uses.

Unravel customer behaviour to enable purposeful engagement and adoption.

Great founders are scientists:

The role of the entrepreneur mirrors that of the scientist. Develop hypotheses, stop over-thinking and start experimenting to find that nugget of value.

In a sense, the entrepreneurial venture itself is an experiment.

Great founders are salespeople:

An entrepreneur's first and last question is "How can I make the next sale?" Especially when you're starting a new business, selling must be your primary job.

Sell yourself, sell your product or service to the press, sell your vision to investors, sell to employees and, most importantly, to your customers.

Great founders are storytellers:

Storytelling is a very powerful tool when engaging a market. A good storyteller articulates not only the offer, they also engage, inspire and convince.

There is no sale without a story.

Great founders are visionaries:

Everyone sees problems, every day, everywhere. The person who sees a solution is a visionary: the person who does something about it is an entrepreneur.
Success is not about how much money you will make: it's about how many people's lives you will change for the better. Real success is experienced when you do things that had never been done before.

So be ambitious and think in orders of magnitude.

Tell Stories

Listen · · Understand

Care · · Experiment

Envision · · Sell

Common Mistakes

- Too much "minimum" in MVP;

- Technology in search of a problem;

- Comparing your beginning to someone else's middle;

- Believing you have no competitors;

- Hiring (lots of) resources before finding Product/Market fit;

- A bet on new human behaviour;

- Building a pitch, not a business;

- Thinking more than 6-12 months ahead;

- Giving stuff away free;

- Not building credibility beyond the internet;

- Building features customers say they want (but won't actually use).

What Matters and What Does Not at the Problem / Solution Stage

Things that matter:

- Finding the right problem and market;

- Over delivering during the first 100 days to new customers;

- Adoption of the product/service;

- 90 % of entrepreneurship is sales;

- Adapting your MVP to market reality;

- Enough "viable" in MVP;

- Spending-a-little-to-learn-a-lot;

- Seeking to understand before you seek to be understood;

- Getting an early "No";

- Not running out of money;

- Focusing on quality over quantity;

- Speed of product & execution.

Things that don't matter:

- What technology you use;

- A business plan;

- Participating in startup contests;

- Talking to strategic "partners";

- Press coverage;

- Adding features;

- Pitching investors;

- Having a focus;

- Having an office;

- Having a logo;

- Having a patent.

Quotes to Live by

We do not learn from experience, we learn from reflecting on experience.

John Dewey

Perfection is achieved, not when you have nothing left to add, but nothing left to take away

Antoine de Saint-Exupery

Simplicity changes behaviour.

BJ Fogg

The only way to win is to learn faster than anyone else.

Eric Ries

I don't measure a man's success by how high he climbs, but how high he bounces back when he hits the bottom.

General Patton

Strive not to be a success, but rather to be of value.
If your product is indeed a value, you'll have a far better chance of being a success.

Unknown

Simplicity is the ultimate sophistication.

Leonardo da Vinci

Design is not just what it looks like and feels like. Design is how it works.

Steve Jobs

If there is no struggle, there is no progress.

Frederick Douglass

To attain knowledge, add things every day. To attain wisdom, remove things every day.

Lao-tse

If you want truly to understand something, try to change it.

Kurt Lewin

Success is the ability to go from failure to failure without losing your enthusiasm.

Winston Churchill

Life is too short to make things no one wants.

Ash Maurya

Coming together is a beginning; keeping together is progress; working together is success.

Henri Ford

Recommended Reading

Buying a $ 25 book is the best investment ever, as you get access to leading practice, years of experience and insights for just a "mosquito price". These three books are extremely helpful at the Problem/Solution phase:

Hooked
Nir Eyal

Hooked is a guide to building habit-forming technology.

Running Lean
Ash Maurya

Iterate from Plan A to A Plan That Works.

Product Management
Intercom

Guidance on the tough decisions you need to make to manage product.

"Invest in duplicating your few strong areas instead of fixing all of your weaknesses."

— Tim Ferriss, Author,
Entrepreneur and Angel Investor

Section 25
Conclusions

Why Silicon Valley Is Better than Hollywood

Tens of thousands of people, believing themselves to be uniquely gifted and talented, move to Los Angeles every year to become famous actors. Very few of them actually become famous actors or stars. Most of them end up as bartenders, waiters or taxi drivers until they leave the city, disappointed.

But founders have their own faith at hand. In Silicon Valley, and for that matter anywhere in the world, it's up to you to make it happen. And if you fail, fail forward. Failing is nothing more than the process of learning. Startup founders support one another because of the unique "pay it forward" mentality. This is unlike actors who are competing for each role in a zero-sum game. For startups, a high tide lifts all boats.

Don't Be Afraid to Kill Your Darlings

At the Problem/Solution Fit stage, it's about framing and nailing the solution. At this stage it's about learning, not earning. You want to verify that your product or service is adopted by the target segment. Early adopters vote for your product or service with their money and time.

Irrespective of what kind of business you plan to launch, good service is what every customer will expect. You don't want to be another cool startup, you want to create a business for the long term. Be passionate about a very long journey ahead of you (5 to 10 years) more than the money.

Don't talk to strategic "partners" at this stage, particularly if they are big. It's a waste of time. Prove your own market and negotiate from a position of strength. Remember, nothing breeds success like success.

It's bad advice to focus at the Problem / Solution Fit stage, as you don't yet know what to focus on. Formulate hypotheses and experiment, experiment, experiment.
It's better to be roughly right than precisely wrong. Don't be afraid to kill your darlings.

Exit Goals for the
Problem / Solution Fit Stage

1. You've framed the problem / need which a customer wants solving.

2. Your hypotheses are validated through experimentation.

3. Your product or service is 10x better than the alternative.

4. Your product or service turns customers into superheroes.

5. You understand customers' behaviour in relation to your product or service.

6. You identified a specific niche of early adopters.

7. You formulated the value proposition as a single clear, compelling and concise message.

8. You explored the first steps towards value-capture.

"Things may come to those who wait... but only the things left by those who hustle."

— Abraham Lincoln,
US President

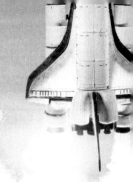

Section 26
Cheat Sheet

Top 50 Developers Stack

Leverage APIs when building an MVP

GitHub
jQuery
Google Analytics
Node.js
Bootstrap
Rails Slack
Heroku
MongoDB
AngularJS
nginx
Redis
Trello
DigitalOcean
JavaScript
New Relic
Git
MySQL

Python
Amazon
EC2
Sublime
Text PHP
Ruby
Google Apps
Docker
PostgreSQL
Dropbox
S3
Stripe
Codeship
Bitbucket
Sass
MailChimp
Java

MEAN
Google Drive
Mandrill
Amazon
CloudFront
Travis
CI Meteor
Pingdom
HipChat
WordPress
Django
Vagrant
Firebase
Kato Gulp
CoffeeScript
Bower

* Source: stackshare.io

Practical Tools

inspectlet.com
Record and monitor how users use your product

foundrs.com
Equity & stock calculator for cofounders

domainr.com
Find the best possible domain names fast

99designs.com
Curated marketplace for creating marketing assets

quantcast.com
Explore age, gender, interest & related sites for any site

wufoo.com
Build powerful online forms quickly

phonegap.com
Create cross-platform mobile apps

fiverr.com
Marketplace offering tasks and services for $ 5

upwork.com
Marketplace for freelancers and remote workers

moovly.com
Create animated videos and presentations

"Some people feel the rain, others just get wet."

— Unknown

Numeri:
Product/Market Fit

Section 27
The Startup Lifecycle

"A satisfied customer
is the best strategy of all."

— Michael Leboeuf, Author

The Shift from Value-Creation to Value-Capture

Ideas don't create value until they're embedded in a product or service. Going from an idea to a product or service is the scope of this third book part: Numeri. This is the stage at which a company goes from 0 to 1, as Peter Thiel calls it.

Going from 0 to 1 is about growing a product.

Growing a product doesn't mean shutting yourself away in a basement to create a product or service. As a startup, you don't want to create a product - you want to create a business.
Interacting with customers is as important, if not more so, than creating a great product or service. This process of customer interaction is called "sales".

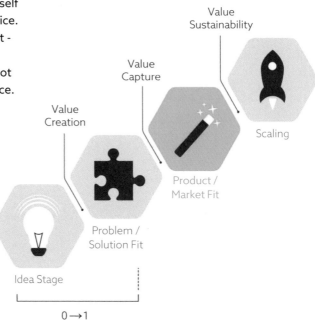

Value Sustainability

Value Capture

Value Creation

Scaling

Product / Market Fit

Problem / Solution Fit

Idea Stage

0 → 1
Cash Preservation

The Company-Building Stage

And sales matters as much as the product in creating a business, as it's seldom the technology that fails. So don't worry about engineering, worry about getting users and customers. No product or service captures value until you embed it in a business model. No business model becomes sustainable until you've figured out distribution.

Going from 1 to n is about growing a market.

Product/market fit is about wrapping up the validation stage. Without a positive outcome, you shouldn't move on to the next stage of scaling. At this stage you're ready to shift your focus from product to distribution in order to "conquer the market".

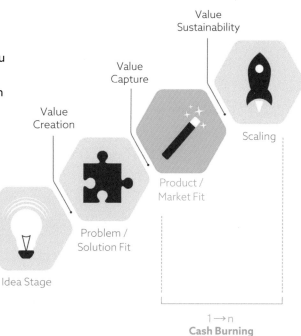

"If you want to make God laugh, tell him about your plans."

— Russian Proverb

Section 28
Product/Market Fit

The Only Thing That Matters Is Getting to Product/Market Fit

The phrase 'Product/Market fit' was popularised by Marc Andreessen in a lecture at Stanford University back in 2007. Andreessen described it as "you know it when you've got it", but that definition doesn't really help.

Ask yourself the question: "Is my product appealing enough to the market to gain significant traction and scale?". Remember, you can't force customers to want, need or like your product. By "product", here we mean all interactions and experiences a user has with the company. You need to offer great onboarding and support so that customers acquire the necessary knowledge, skills and behaviour to use the service with the least friction possible.

Let's see what startup thought leaders have to say about that magic moment of product/market fit.

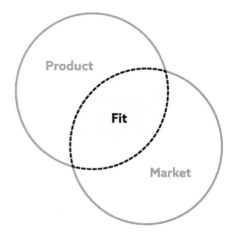

Thought Leaders on Product/Market Fit

"Product/market fit means being in a good market with a product that can satisfy that market."
Marc Andreessen
A16Z, Venture Capital Firm

"Poor conversions, no word-of-mouth, slow usage growth, long sales cycle, and high churn."
Carlos Espinal
Seed Camp

"If you need to ask whether you have product/market fit, the answer is simple: you don't."
Eric Ries
The Lean Startup

"Figure out value first before growth."
Ash Maurya
Running Lean

"Business-model realisation is part of the product/market fit."
Steve Blank
Customer Development

"Make things people want."
Paul Graham
Y Combinator

"If there is no retention and referrals, there's no product/market fit."
Dave McClure
500 Startups

"At least 40 % of users saying they would be very disappointed without your product."
Sean Ellis
GrowthHackers

"Think in reverse: market/product fit, not product/market fit."
Alistar Croll & Ben Yoskovitz
Lean Analytics

"Product-Market fit is the level of match between what customers want and what a product provides."
Matt Brocchini
QPMF

"$ 0 of MRR: no P/M fit
$ 1 to $ 10k MRR: illusion
$ 10k to $ 100k MRR: a semblance
$ 100k to $ 500k MRR: sweet spot"
Brad Feld
Foundry Group

Product/Market Fit or Escaping Gravity

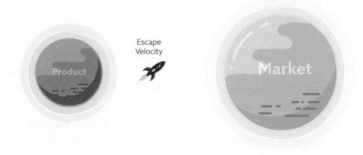

Product/market fit is shifting the focus from building a product to winning the market. In other words, product/market fit is the transition from "proof of product" to "proof of market". Escaping the gravity that keeps a startup small by proving and extracting value from the market is the mission of every business.

The Importance of Product/Market Fit

Growth solves all problems: a lack of growth cannot be solved by anything other than growth. However, growth should not kill you, but rather empower you. You can't grow something that sucks. You might be able to attract a huge number of users, but they will not stick around for long if the experience is poor. Understand how they use the product, and how it satisfies their needs.

First think in terms of customer commitment rather than growth. So create something sticky before pouring fuel on the fire by figuring out the sales process. Delivering sustainable customer value prevails over accelerating user acquisition.

It's frustrating to work at a startup that's struggling to find a product/market fit. On the other hand, if you are scaling too quickly, you'll burn up capital and destroy your team. Unfortunately, you can't set a deadline on product/market fit. Remember that a startup operates in conditions of extreme uncertainty.

Product/market fit is the point where you can aim the product/service for a specific type of customer. Before product/market fit, there is no point in focusing—it should be the opposite—go broad: throw a lot of stuff out at a high speed to see what sticks.

From Andreessen's definition of product/market fit—being in a good market with a product which will satisfy that market— it follows that having found product/market fit in too small a market is a dead-end for your startup. The target market (niche) needs to be big enough to create and support a sustainable business.

The methodology you apply, whether it's the lean startup, business-model canvas or customer development, is less relevant. As long as users do care and perceive the product or the service as a "must-have" rather than a "nice-to-have". Once you've figured out the product/market fit, just add water, i.e. throw VC money, marketing pundits and MBAs at it.

The Difference Between Traction and Growth

Traction entails a thorough understanding of user behaviour, enabling you to improve the product or service.

A small but steady stream of users allows you to iterate and improve based on data instead of assumptions. Traction allows you to fine-tune the value proposition to a well-defined target user. To generate initial traction, you will need to acquire almost every customer "manually", so forget about automation and figure out what you can do manually. Invest in traction, but don't invest in growth too soon before you have retention, as you're renting users, not acquiring them.

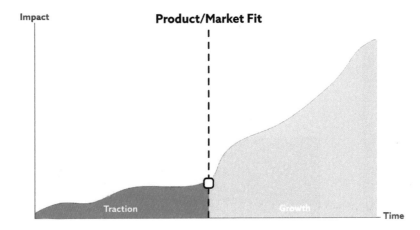

Growth on the other hand is about finding various levers, i.e. scalable and repeatable engines, to boost user acquisition in a cost-effective way.

knowledge that your fundamentals are tried-and-tested. However, don't confuse (early) traction with product/market fit.

Growth without traction can kill your business. Growing your customer base and building your momentum slowly but surely— secure in the

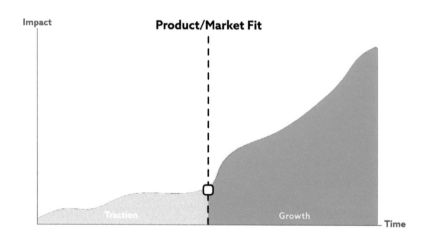

What Is Scaling?

The chart below explains scaling using 2 axes:

External growth axis is about finding and acquiring customers —i.e. go-to-market activities such as sales, marketing, pricing, going international etc.

Internal growth axis is about maturity of the organisation — i.e. hiring talent, finding funding, legal stuff, financial stuff, technology stack, etc.

The trend areas (green and turquoise) are scenarios of various scaling speeds. For each company, this trend line will be a unique fingerprint.

The combination of balanced internal and external growth is key to successful scaling.

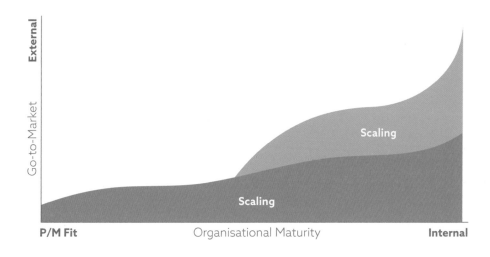

The Danger of Premature Scaling

Premature scaling is the #1 predictor of failure. According to the Startup Genome report, after analysing 3,200 startups, 70 % of startups fail through premature scaling. Premature scaling overstretches a startup's ability to execute.

The most common mistake is to confuse a few early adopters with a market. As a consequence, overspending too much on customer acquisition, hiring too many employees and raising too much money too early, can be lethal.

Product/Market Fit Is the Difference Between a Startup and a Scale-up

Startup	Product/Market Fit	Scaleup
Market Exploration		Market Exploitation
Search		Execute
Create Value		Capture Value
Experiment		Focus
Uncushioned Customer Contact		Process Driven Customer Contact
Competition From Startups		Competition From Incumbents
Product Building		Company Building
MVP		Robust Stack
Early Adopters		Majority
Feature Poor		Technical Debt
Bootstrapping & Grants		Venture Capital
Pivoting		Optimizing
Founding Team		Formal Roles
Effectiveness		Efficiency
Pre-PM		Post-PM

"You cannot paint Mona Lisa by assigning one dab each to a thousand painters."

— William F. Buckley, Jr,
Author

Section 29

Quantifying and Qualifying Product/Market Fit

The Foundations of Every Business

The fundamentals of any business are essentially the same: it's about acquiring, serving and retaining customers.

You can see a striking similarity with a sports game: offence gets you in the game (i.e. sales) whereas defence wins championships (i.e. serve and retain). The successful combination of these three activities will lead to repeat customers, a sure sign that you've nailed the product offering. Product/market fit should reflect these three key activities, as we will see in the next slides.

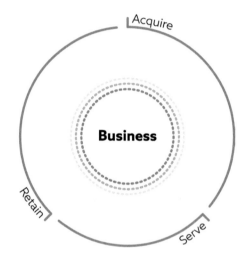

Get Better, Not Bigger

Reaching the product/market fit stage is about getting better, not bigger. It's not the number of customers that's important, but their weight, i.e. repeat usage, consumption and stickiness.

So don't count how many customers you have; rather, weigh your impact on them. A small but loyal customer base will facilitate healthy, retention-based growth. It's like compound interest: there is no stronger force in economics. The value of software is in proportion to not only the size, but more particularly the engagement, of users. Unsurprisingly, retention- based growth is directly proportional to providing customers with what they need.

A focus on service and support could be more of a key differentiator than the actual core-product. According to Bain & Company, a customer is four times more likely to defect to a competitor if the problem is service-related than price- or product-related.

Before getting to the product/market fit stage, you will probably need to pivot 1-2 times and it might take six months to two years. Then you might find a product/market fit.

Product/Market Fit Requirements

There are three "must-have" requirements in order to achieve a product/market fit:

1. Retention rate at least 20 %-40 %;

2. Identified and tested at least three growth engines;

3. Robustness to handle the next order of magnitude of growth;

And two optional requirements: (1) demonstrate a viable business model and (2) validate pricing.

Remember that the product/market fit represents the validation stage. Without a positive outcome to these requirements, you shouldn't move to the next stage of scaling. They are simply an essential condition.

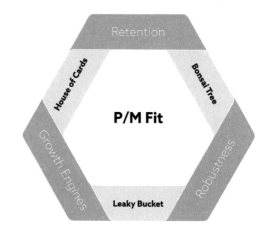

Acquisition represents the level of eagerness from customers whereas retention equals affection of the market for your product. Robustness is the level of maturity of the organization to handle scaling.

Requirement 1: Retention

The finest metric for product/market fit is a must-have-product. That's way more important than virality. Sharing a funny cats video doesn't make it a must-have-product or service. Virality is not a good proxy for sustainability. However, customers who have been retained over a long time are more likely to promote your product or service. Simply put, leaky buckets don't need more water. They need their holes fixed.

First think in terms of customer commitment rather than financials. Delivering sustainable customer value prevails over short-term value extraction. Get your product into the hands of customers. Understand how they use it, and how it satisfies their needs.

The minimum threshold is that 20 %, ideally 40 %, of your customers/users should perceive your product or service as a must-have rather than a nice-to-have.

Although this might look low, it's likely that in the early MVP days, only a specific segment of the target market will show high retention, while other segments will have a high churn.

Within the 20 %-40 % of high-retention customers, look at how they interact with your product, service and company. Understand their industry, their size, how they are using your product, what geographical location they are in etc.

For a business-to-business company, 10 customers/users are sufficient as a sample size – i.e. 2 to 4 customers/users who perceive the product or service as a must-have, or even business critical, is enough for now. For business-to-consumer (B2C), a sample size of 100 consumers is recommended, with at least 20 of them perceiving it as a must-have in order to fulfill their needs.

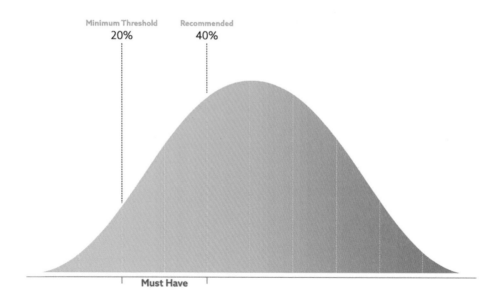

Retention Trumps Growth

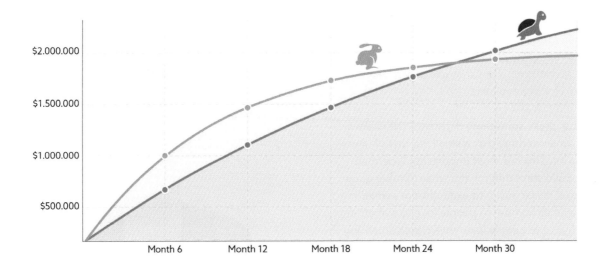

Consider two companies: Hare and Tortoise. Hare generates new revenue of $ 200,000 per month, while Tortoise generates $ 100,000 per month. Hare has a monthly retention rate of 90 %, while Tortoise has a monthly retention rate of 97 %.

Despite the growth rate of Hare, twice as high as Tortoise, in the long run retention trumps growth. Acquisition on its own doesn't equal growth.

Retention
Sam Altman's View of Retention

It's much easier to expand from something that a small number of people love to something that a lot of people love, as opposed to expanding from something a lot of people like to something a lot of people love.

You can make something that many users like a little, or something that a small number of users love a lot. This is a most important piece of advice. Build something that a small number of users love. It's far easier to expand from something that a small number of people love to something which a lot of people love, than from something that a lot of people like to one which a lot of people love. If you get it right, you can then afford to get a lot of other things wrong. However, if you don't get this right, even if you get everything else right you will probably still fail.

Requirement 2: Growth Engines

Until you reach P/M fit, you'll need to acquire almost every customer manually. There is no need to focus on automation or scalable growth engines just yet. But as well as having a sticky product, you also need to overcome the sales challenge: finding a customer with unit economics that make sense (i.e. the direct costs associated with a particular growth engine are lower than the generated gross margin). Simply put, a growth engine should bring in more money than the sales & marketing budget you invest in it.

You may have designed a great car, but without fuel it won't move an inch. Having great retention on your product or service but failing to acquire customers in a cost-effective way is failing to reach product/market fit, because you can't begin to scale your business just yet. This is a tough challenge, especially for founders with a technical background.

However, sales is not an art or magic that's mastered by a happy few. The reality is, it's a science, therefore it can be approached and set-up as a process. There are many tips and tricks in this area, and while they might bring you a few leads, they will not cut it to drive sustainable growth. Think like an architect rather than a salesperson. The agility of sprints applied to sales processes will help you to find the right way to go, and fast.

Needless to say, working multiple growth engines are an important aspect to investors. If you can show you're able to scale the business by increasing the sales and marketing budget, you make for an attractive investment. The lower the cost of acquisition is in relation to revenue, or more precisely profit, the better your business is at capturing and extracting value from the market.

Identify 3-5 Growth Engines

Even after you've found a way to acquire customers with positive economic units, you still need to find more acquisition methods in order to reach potential buyers. Depending on the bandwidth of the team, at least 3 and up to 5 growth engines need to be identified and tested.

Why do you need multiple growth engines? Because:

Growth doesn't come out of a magic bullet. You need 3-5 engines in order to take off. Customer acquisition is the result of a successful combination of different marketing and sales activities.

Growth engines have a lifetime, and inflation will kick in at some stage. Especially in a digital world with an ever increasing clock speed

Combining multiple growth engines leads to more rapid growth. For a startup to take off, just like an aeroplane it needs multiple growth engines to get airborne.

Growth Engines
Kill, Iterate/Pivot or Scale

There is much debate about going deep when testing growth engines versus going wide. Ideally, growth engines need to be tested in 2-week sprints. Decide after the sprint whether to (1) kill, (2) iterate/pivot or (3) scale the growth engine.

This works fine for online marketing such as e-mail, content marketing, social media, PR or SEA. It also works for outbound calling, even when sales cycles are longer than 2 weeks, because the conversion rates and velocity of the pipeline provide early indicators of potentially successful growth engines.

Even for attending exhibitions or face-to-face meetings, a sprint of 2 weeks focusing on follow-up activities provides strong indicators of the potential performance of those growth engines.

As an important aside: loyal customers cost more to get, so take this into account when assessing performance.

Growth Engines
The Bottom of the Funnel Is More Important

Finding a viable acquisition channel with profitable unit economics calls for ample testing, as it typically takes 3 to 5 sprints to identify a successful growth engine.

Although it sounds counterintuitive, don't focus on "filling" the top of the sales funnel with a lot of leads. At this stage, that's rather a vanity metric. Focus your attention on the bottom-of-the-funnel, where potential customers are at the point of purchase. For instance, sales success isn't about the number of cold calls you make, it's about the results you achieve. Focus on customers who will convert within the next 2 weeks, and master the process of conversion. Once that process is established, experiment with the middle and then the top of the funnel.

The three parameters that define funnel performance are reach, conversion and velocity. Note that the funnel is drawn from left to right, not from top to bottom, in order to avoid the perception that, once reach is successful (say website traffic), revenue will automatically come out, as if gravity would drag leads down. Nothing could be farther from the truth: every stage in the funnel needs to be carefully designed in order to ensure conversion.

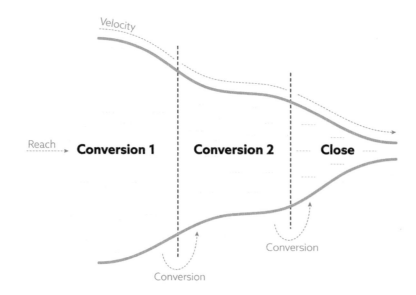

Requirement 3: Robustness

Unlike retention and growth engines, which are quantified in terms of percentages and numbers respectively, robustness is qualified and expressed rather as a domain or process.

Since product/market fit is readiness to scale, one has to ask: What will happen if we have 10x more users or customers? What will break or create friction? Will it be the product stack? Onboarding? Customer service? Supply chain? Servers? etc. Once you have the answer and you know how to tackle the looming issues, you have the robustness needed to handle the next magnitude of scaling.

Asking what will happen when 10x more customers join the platform is a never-ending powerful issue during scaling.

Usually, robustness-related challenges are in two main domains represented by the horizontal, internal growth axis on the scale graph:

- Technology: is it scalable, i.e. having the ability to add significant number of users without running into stability or performance issues, or requiring re-engineering?

- Organisation: people are not scalable, often additional team-members are required in customer-facing positions such as customer onboarding, service and success.

Product/Market Fit Recommendations

Frame the Business Model

Although not strictly a requirement, it is advisable to test your business model, paying special attention to the way value will be captured. While it's true that keeping adding users fast and figuring out how to monetise it later works for certain businesses — think Facebook — is possible, those companies are outliers with deep-pocketed VCs on board.

Frame the Pricing

Pricing is one the major challenges every startup faces. The main reason why it is advisable to validate your pricing at this stage is simple: the price your customers are willing to pay is the measure of the extent to which you've nailed the solution.

After Product/Market Fit
Venture Capital

Once you reach product/market fit, it's a good moment to assess the prospects of raising money. Money becomes cheaper once you've reached product/market fit, in the same way fuel is cheap but building a car is not. Fund-raising is not easy, yet it's a time-consuming activity that may be necessary for scaling. However, if the three product/market fit conditions (retention, growth engines and robustness) are met, combined with a big enough target market, it should be a smoother process.

Spare the time to practice your pitch deck. If you can't express it simply and clearly, keep working at it till you can. Even top-comedians need months of preparation for a 15-minute act. A pitch deck is a way of articulating your ambitions as a coherent narrative, backed up by numbers. VCs are smart, and they are essentially gamblers trying to hedge their bets. Proving that you have reached product/market fit using the methodology described in this Masterclass is de-risking the investment for the investors, and therefore they have an incentive to move in fast, before it becomes more expensive to join.

Raise funds based on milestones, not runway.

After Product/Market Fit
Advisory Board

Remember when experience mattered? The lessons when scaling companies are always the same. An Advisory Board is the fast lane to experience. The fastest way to know how to use a new device is by having somebody who is experienced to explain it to you instead of reading a manual from cover to cover.

An Advisory Board is an often-overlooked, under-utilised, or completely overlooked lever for high-growth companies. An Advisory Board is particularly useful for first-time entrepreneurs, or for founding teams who lack a substantial amount of domain or market experience. Especially for fast-growing businesses, the danger of outstripping the founding team's capabilities is real. If entrepreneurship is a battle, most casualties stem from friendly fire or self-inflicted wounds.

Not only do Advisory Boards anticipate problems and provide answers, they also make introductions and push founders hard. And perhaps the most valuable part: they provide an outsider's view. When you're inside the bottle, it's hard to read the label. That's why companies with an advisory board attract investors more easily, perform better and are less likely to fail.

A well-managed Advisory Board can help open doors, keep you on track, and avoid common company-killing errors.

Be a tortoise, first and foremost
It's better to be a tortoise (high retention) than a hare (high growth). However, the exceptional combination of both is a unicorn.

"Be sure you put your feet in
the right place, then stand firm."

— Abraham Lincoln,
President of the United States

Section 30

Product/Market Fit Myths

Myths About Product/Market Fit

Duncan Watts, author of the popular book 'Six Degrees', describes a phenomenon in complex systems called 'phase transition'. Phase transition is an abrupt step-change as opposed to gradual change. The example he used is magnets—from one moment to the next they become instantly magnetic. Once a tipping-point is reached, the entire system changes. Phase transitions occur at the upper and lower boundaries of complex systems such as chemical reactions, organisations and ecosystems.

One of the major myths is that product/market fit is a phase transition that will change everything overnight. Although it's true that the impact is huge, don't expect a big bang at a discrete point in time. Often, you will achieve (partly) product/market fit for a specific segment or geographical area.

There was a lively discussion on the subject between rock-star venture capitalists Fred Wilson of Union Square Ventures and Ben Horowitz of A16Z. You'll find an extract from the main points made by Ben Horowitz in this section.

Lastly, there are also non-believers. According to them, there is no such thing as product/market fit. An interesting view on the subject comes from Evernote's CEO, as we shall see towards the end of this section.

Product/Market Fit Is Always a Discrete, Big Bang Event

Some companies achieve primary product market fit in a big bang. Most however don't: instead they get there through partial fits, a few false alarms, and a big dollop of perseverance.

By the time it got acquired, Opware had achieved product market fit for a category of software called data-centre automation. But it wasn't at all obvious that was going to be our destination while we were getting there. We actually achieved product market fit in a number of smaller sub-markets such as Unix server automation for service-providers, then Unix server automation for enterprise data-centres, then Windows server automation, and eventually network automation and process automation. Along the way, we also built a few products that never found product/market fit.

Similarly, Joel Spolsky of Joel on Software and Fog Creek Software fame has an exciting new company called Stack Overflow. He achieved product/market fit in the collaboratively-edited Q&A market for audiences such as software engineers and mathematicians.

Is this the primary product market fit? Neither of those markets seems that large. Will he need significant new features to find the big product market fit? Probably. Should he invest or stay lean? Good question, but there's no formulaic answer.

Ben Horowitz

* Source: www.bhorowitz.com/revenge_of_the_fat_guy

It's Patently Obvious When You Have Product/Market Fit

I'm sure Twitter knew when it achieved product market fit, but it's far murkier for most startups. How many customers (or site visitors or monthly active users or booked revenue dollars, etc.) must you have to prove the point? As I previously mentioned, there may be multiple sub-markets, each of which needs their own product. I show below that Fred himself didn't realise Loudcloud had achieved product market fit, even though we had. It's not usually black and white.

Or let's try a consumer products example. Apple's first iPod shipped in November 2001. It took nearly two years (91 weeks, to be precise) to sell its first million units. In contrast, Apple's iPhone 3GS shipped June 2009 and shipped one million units in 3 days. At what point is it obvious to the original iPod team that they've achieved product/market fit?

Ben Horowitz

* Source: www.bhorowitz.com/revenge_of_the_fat_guy

Once You Achieve It, You Cannot Lose It

Fred implies that we raised a shedload of money for Loudcloud before achieving product market fit. That is not so. Four months after founding Loudcloud, we had already booked $ 12M in customer contracts, so we had product/market fit by most measures. I'd defy any VC, including Fred, to point to a company with a $ 36M run rate 4 months after founding where the VC advised "Stay lean until you achieve product/market fit."

But after that bolt out of the starting gate, the market for cloud services changed dramatically. After Exodus went bankrupt in September 2001, the market for cloud services from semi-viable companies went to zero and we lost product/market fit as a cloud service-provider. We had to rebuild completely and would ultimately find product/market fit in a different set of markets altogether.

Ben Horowitz

* Source: www.bhorowitz.com/revenge_of_the_fat_guy

MYTH 4

Once You Have It, You Don't Have to Sweat the Competition

It's fine to stay lean if you're not quite sure that you have product/market fit and there are no competitors in your face every day. But usually there are. In fact, the best markets are usually those in which competition is fierce because the opportunity is big. How long should you stay lean before attacking? Again, there is no formula that will work in all (or even most) cases.

Ben Horowitz

* Source: www.bhorowitz.com/revenge_of_the_fat_guy

Evernote Founder Phil Libin: Product/Market Fit Is Bullshit

At an interview at the Web Summit in Dublin, Libin said that Evernote's own staff remain the main test group for new features, and warned startup founders to trust their own instincts more when coming up with a new digital service.

"We make things we love. I think that's critical. Product/market fit is [kind of] a bullshit concept. You can't approach it that way: 'What should I build? Let me go and see what the market needs!'. That doesn't make any sense: your only competitive advantage is to make something great," Libin said. "How are you going to make something great unless you make it for yourself? How are you even [going to] know that it's great? You make something you love, and then you find the market that it fits."

That was said on 4 November 2014. 2 weeks later, after they released a new version that drew massive complaints, Evernote issued this communication: "We're sorry. We screwed up. We've heard your feedback, and are going to make things better".

"Early revenue isn't the inflection point it used to be. You can always find a few paying customers."

— Tim Ferriss, Author

Section 31
Validating the Business Model

What Is a Business Model?

In essence, a business model is an answer to how an organisation sustains itself financially. In order to survive and thrive, organisations need to have a viable business model. A business model is the structure that comprises every aspect of a company, including creating, delivering and capturing value, and describes how they all work together.

In the words of Peter Drucker: "A business model is nothing more or less than a representation of how an organisation makes (or intends to make) money."

There are three common ways to make (more) money out of the paying customer:

1. Get more customers → Attract or convert more
2. Keep more customers → Increase retention
3. Earn more per customer → Increase price

But making money is just one, albeit important, part of a business model. Monetising data, creating network effects, becoming hyper-scalable, raising capital, having a talented team, creating partnerships and taking the top position in a winner-takes-almost-all market can be equally or even more important for building a successful business.

The business model chosen also impacts the go-to-market and customer service approach, and therefore the organisation's design. Competition increasingly takes place not between products, but among business models. So it's worth spending some time on the subject.

If you're using Alexander Osterwalder's Business Model Canvas or Ash Maurya's Lean Canvas, product/market fit can be defined as the point at which value proposition, customer segments and channels are fixed, without requiring any additional pivots.

Note that creating a canvas is not sufficient in itself, nor does it represent all dimensions of your business model. Many key factors for success are not covered on the canvas. For instance retention, robustness and pricing are crucial for success; so is cash-flow. And you need a growth strategy in order to realise the full potential of a business model.

PROBLEM	SOLUTION	UNIQUE VALUE PROPOSITION	UNFAIR ADVANTAGE	CUSTOMER SEGMENTS
	KEY METRICS		CHANNELS	
COST STRUCTURE		REVENUE STREAMS		

Characteristics of a Hyper-Scalable Business Model

1. Creates a competitive advantage through a Network Effect (i.e. Metcalfe's law);

2. Has built-in virality, so your customers do your marketing for you;

3. Has the potential to create a natural monopoly;

4. Doesn't need to manage inventory;

5. Doesn't need a supply chain;

6. Has a cost of goods sold (COGS) of less than 5 % of revenue;

7. Is based on intangible assets (IP, data, algorithms, patents, etc);

8. Is capex light;

9. Can become a platform acting as the foundation for an entire ecosystem;

10. "Pay up-front" cash-flow model (i.e. collect money before the service is delivered);

11. Unit economics that improve as scale increases;

12. Self-service or low-touch service;

13. Two-pizza team size for the core team, avoiding the Ringelmann effect;

14. Benefits from Moore's law (viability) and Koomey's law (feasibility).

Different Business Models

The wrong question to ask is: Which business model should I use? Rather ask yourself first: Why will people pay me? Once you've figured out the answer—i.e. the value proposition—it's time to figure out how best to capture that value. This is where different business models come in.

There are various business models, such as transactional-based, subscription-based, two-sided marketplaces, consumption based, auction model, affiliate model, franchising, monetisng of data, in-app revenue, API-first, crowdsourced-based, community-riven, donation-based, open-source, all-you-can-eat, pay what you want, freemium, etc. Two popular up-and-coming business models are the subscription-based model and the two-sided marketplace model. We will cover each in greater detail.

The Subscription Business Model

Subscription-based business models are growing in popularity thanks to technology acting as an enabler (cloud and mobile) and shifting socio-economic trends (changing consumer preferences driven by millennials), thereby giving rise to the subscription economy.

The subscription model is a business model whereby a customer must pay a subscription fee to gain access to the product/service. At the core of the subscription model is the customer relationship, not the product or service. Subscriptions are in essence forward-looking revenue models. The keyword is regular.

Renewal of a subscription may be periodic and activated automatically, so that the cost of a new period is paid automatically by a pre-authorised charge to a credit card or checking account.

Subscription models are not new, but thanks to technology they are exploding in all kinds of industries: printed media, culture, cleaning and gardening services, books, meals, pet-food, insurance, public transport, charity, software, music, movies, clothing, education, navigation systems, coffee, fitness clubs, telecoms and shaving products. 23andMe even tried to put DNA-checks-as-a-subscription on the market in 2012, but that attempt failed.

Shifting from selling products to managing relationships means not only a new approach to revenue growth, but also a new way to measure success. Unlike one-off purchase models, in which vendors have no incentive to maintain relationships with their customers (think real-estate or the automotive industry), subscription models align customers and vendors toward common goals. Subscription models force the company to keep in touch and engage with their customers. The latter challenge is not simple, but subscription models have another benefit that helps them to stay engaged: it enables them to gather substantial amounts of information from customers.

Subscription-Model Categories

	Financial	Usage	Unit
All You Can Eat Amazon	Limited	Unlimited	Infrequent
Pay-as-You-Go Utilities	Unlimited	Unlimited	Infrequent
Flat Fee SaaS	Limited	Limited	Frequent
Free Media/Samplings	N/A	Limited	Frequent

In the first scenario, a customer will pay the provider a set amount for unlimited access to a product or service delivered over time. The second scenario is consumption-driven. The third scenario provides a fixed service or product for a predefined amount. And finally, the fourth type of subscription model is one in which free sampling or free access is offered, often as a teaser and in exchange for data and feedback.

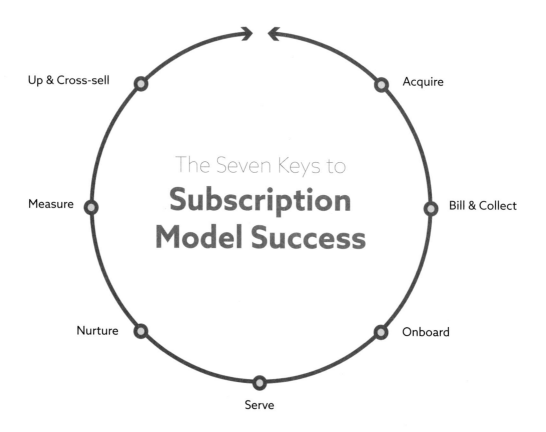

The Seven Keys to
**Subscription
Model Success**

Up & Cross-sell

Acquire

Measure

Bill & Collect

Nurture

Onboard

Serve

Subscription Models Are a Win-Win for Both Buyer and Seller

Buyer

- The value lies in the convenience;

- Autopilot simplicity of subscriptions (no thinking);

- No need to remember to reorder;

- Subscriptions often give a flat rate, which helps customers to keep within their budget;

- Brings added value to the customer through bundling or getting everything for the price of one;

Seller

- It reduces uncertainty and riskiness;

- Reliable forecast (and therefore fundable);

- Higher average customer lifetime value (ACLV) than that of non-recurring business models;

- High switching cost means greater customer inertia;

- Prepayment and simplicity of pricing;

- Data to generate customer insight;

- Planning (inventory & resources);

- Greater potential for upselling and cross-selling;

- Building relationships is a competitive advantage;

Two-Sided Marketplaces

The Internet was supposed to cut out the middleman. To a certain extent, that's exactly what happened. But the Internet became the new intermediary. Unsurprisingly, the marketplace approach is the leading business model for scale-ups in Europe, accounting for 25 % of all business models.

A two-sided marketplace is a platform that brings two parties (sellers and buyers) together for direct interaction and transactions. Known brands in that space are eBay, Monster.com, Uber, PayPal and Match.com. Although it's an attractive business model, the two-sided marketplace is notoriously hard to build.

Why are two-sided marketplaces difficult to build? Two reasons:

1. Ensuring that there is both demand and supply;
2. Ensuring that there is liquidity, i.e. the number of products and service exchanged against the total number offered;

In other words, a two-sided marketplace needs to scale both the quantity (offering volume) and the quality (liquidity) within its target group. Liquidity is the single most important indicator for product/market fit.

Most startups need to worry about one side of the market: attracting customers for their services and products. In a two-sided marketplace, you need to attract two sides, in other words the customer acquisition strategy needs to open on two fronts at the same time. It's as if you're building two parallel companies.

Once a startup reaches enough suppliers and buyers–and liquidity–it's hard for a new competitor to break into that space because of the network effect. Size matters! Any startup facing the early challenges of Metcalfe's Law knows the importance of quickly building out their network in order to create value. Once a critical mass is achieved, the supply-and-demand dynamic allows startups to develop attractive algorithms such as dynamic pricing.

If a startup identifies a market segment in which buyers and the sellers are the same, it will be a much easier problem to solve. Etsy and DeviantArt are good examples. People who make handicrafts or art are likely to buy from other people who also make handicrafts or art. Or consider a dating site for straight people where you need to find sufficient profiles of both genders to make it attractive. Compare this with launching a gay dating site. Since the demand and supply is in the same group, a two-sided marketplace problem becomes a single-sided marketplace problem.

Case Study: Airbnb & PayPal

In a two-sided marketplace, the side with higher price sensitivity receives a subsidy in order to stimulate demand from the other side.

Airbnb

The host receives a fee to cover the cost of processing customer payment (subsidy). Why? There are free listing services on the market, which creates a barrier for hosts to pay Airbnb's high listing rates. Buyers are price-sensitive too, but Airbnb is often well below higher-priced market alternatives (e.g. hotels / BnBs).

PayPal

Existing customers receive a subsidy ($ 10) for each new user they recruit. At the same time, those new users also get $ 10. The merchant gets a better deal compared with the transaction costs of credit cards.

"In God we trust; all others must bring data."

— W. Edwards Deming, Author

Section 32

Raising Money after Product/Market Fit

Considering Raising Capital

There are three scenarios when it's easier to raise capital:

1. When there is a big vision and a story of how to get there (typically a large seed);

2. When you have P/M fit (typically series A);

3. When the numbers speak for themselves (typically series B);

Note that "money is way cheaper" once P/M fit is reached. For investors, momentum is currency.

Once product/market fit is reached, it's the moment to consider raising money pushing the accelerator in a specific direction.

Conserve Cash	Invest Aggressively
Searching for Product/Market Fit	Scaling the Business

Fred Wilson's View on Investing Post Product/Market Fit

"I have invested in about 100 web companies. The very best investments I have been involved in established product market fit before raising a lot of money. And the success rate of fat companies versus lean companies is stark. I have never, not once, been successful with an investment in a company that raised a shedload of money before it had found traction and product market fit with its primary product. That's how Geocities did it. That's how Twitter did it. That's how Zynga did it. That's how every single one of my top twenty web investments in my career did it."

Fred Wilson is an American Businessman and Venture Capitalist, cofounder of Union Square Ventures.

Convincing Investors

The core message to investors goes typically as follows: we are solving this (big) problem/need using this (magic) solution in this (large) market with this (super) team.

The points you need to address with investors:

How do we create value? (Problem/Solution Fit)

How do we capture value? (Business Model)

How do we distribute value? (Distribution/G2M)

How do we plan to scale? (Growth engines with positive economic units)

These are our key numbers (Market potential, Cost of sales, margins, retention, ...)

Founder   Investor

Investors will try to validate the investment by assessing:

Is the value proposition clear?

Is the product or service sticky?

Is the business model viable?

Can you execute?

Can you scale?

Is their sustainable advantage?

Is the target market big enough?

Is their a path to valorization?

Purpose of the **Pitch Deck**

The purpose of your pitch deck is not to answer every conceivable question, nor to close immediate investment. The aim is to turn the business potential into an investment proposition that will attract investor's attention and get them keen to know more. You want to give them enough information to arouse their interest, but not so much as to overwhelm them.

Be well aware when framing the investment narrative that an entrepreneur is growth-oriented, but an investor focuses on return (yield). Every investment request presents the ultimate question for investors: is it worth their while to invest their time and money? Or is it just a waste of both? So make investors feel they will regret it if they pass up the opportunity: the rocket will take off with or without them.

The good thing about talking to a venture capitalist is that they bring you down to earth.

Sample Pitch Deck

Slide 1
The Problem

_____

What is the problem?

Define the real problem or need you're solving, and for whom.

Slide 2
Our Solution

_____

Is there a strong offer with a supporting cost of goods?

- Great value at the right price;
- Value proposition;
- Point out the stickiness;

Slide 3
Product Overview

_____

Tell the story of your customer and how customers use/value your product or service.

Images and visuals are better than lots of text: show, don't tell. A live demo is always best.

Slide 4
Our Advantages

_____

Provide an answer to the following questions:

- How is your place in the market unique to you?
- What are your Advantages?
- Where do you fit in the larger overall market?

**Slide 5
The Market**

Define your market: what business/industry you are in, and what's the total addressable market.

Clearly define exactly the personas whom you serve. Give an example of a real customer with a prototypical use case.

**Slide 6
Business Model**

The business model is there to show that you understand the business.

- How do you monetise?
- Key revenue-streams;
- What is the rationale behind pricing?

**Slide 7
Projections**

Provide a glimpse into the future.

- Express the business potential as realistic numbers.
- Include multi-years of financial projections.

**Slide 8
Competition**

Who else is already doing this, how are they going about it and what are they not getting right or doing wrong?

Slide 9
Investment

—————————————

State how much capital you're raising.

What is the use of proceeds? Be well aware that equity is your most precious resource you have. You have something to offer which the other side of the table would like to have.

Slide 10
Our Team

—————————————

Highlight team-members' profiles and previous positions, successes, domain expertise.

Demonstrate relevant experience or education.

Slide 11
Contact

—————————————

Provide contact details.

Take your feedback home. Whatever you did or said, afterwards you will think over what you might have done better. Make sure you write down these after-thoughts so you can adapt your narrative and get better with every iteration.

After all, you're the protagonist in this story, so you'd better learn to tell it well and make it epic.

Bootstrapping Could Be an Option

Startups that went a long way bootstrapping (up to a certain point)

"Come for money when you know what to do with it, not when you run out of it and need it."

— Rokas Tamošiūnas,
Cofounder of StartupHighway

Section 33

Setting Up an Advisory Board

Fact

Companies with an advisory board attract investors more easily, perform better and are less likely to fail.

Why an Advisory Board?

An Advisory Board is an often overlooked, under-utilised, or completely neglected lever for high-growth companies. An Advisory Board is particularly useful for first-time entrepreneurs or for founding teams who lack a substantial amount of domain or market experience. Especially for fast-growing businesses, the danger of outstripping the founding team's capabilities is real. If entrepreneurship is a battle, most casualties stem from friendly fire or self-inflicted wounds.

A well-managed Advisory Board can help open doors, keep you on track, and avoid common company-killing errors. Not only do Advisory Boards anticipate problems and provide answers, they also make introductions and push founders hard. And perhaps the most valuable part: they provide an outsider's view. When you're inside the bottle, it's hard to read the label.

Remember when experience mattered? The lessons in scaling companies are always the same. An Advisory Board is a fast lane to experience. The fastest way to know how to use a new device is by having somebody who is experienced to explain it to you instead of reading a manual from cover to cover.

We have been setting up over 30 Advisory Boards for startups and scale-ups in recent years. In our experience these meetings are simply critical. It's not about discussing financial statements in detail, but it provides the time and space for strategy discussions and to put business challenges on the table. Advisory Boards play a key role during scaling, in challenging times and at a liquidity event.

Once you're convinced your company needs one, it comes down to finding the right people who can make the difference, and persuading them to join.

Typical Questions and Dilemmas Handled by an Advisory Board

- Self-funding versus outside capital;

- Sources of capital;

- Pivot dilemma;

- When hiring who for what;

- Firing;

- Understanding the competition;

- Picking markets, geo & verticals;

- Opening a branch;

- Working with partners;

- Tweaking the business model;

- Collecting and understanding metrics;

- Judging an acquisition offer;

- Handling the board of directors;

- Reviewing pricing.

Why an Advisory Board?

An Advisory Board advises the entrepreneur, not the company. Big difference. If you have nothing but investors, you will have everyone's actions guided by their own financial self-interest. The role of a Board of Directors is to protect shareholders' interests, whereas an Advisory Board works in the interests of a very special shareholder: the founder. The person who holds the key to success or failure.

An Advisory Board has three types of profile:

Accelerator: typically an (ex-)entrepreneur who has gone from zero to at least a double-digit number in revenue.

Enabler: typically a financial, fiscal, legal or executive profile.

Domain Expert: complementary to your skills and experience. Typically deep expertise in technology or vertical industry knowledge.

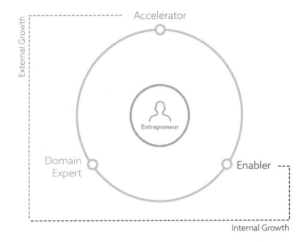

An Accelerator always wants the company to move fast while an enabler has a critical eye for the risks. The Advisory Board should consist of no more than five people to keep it manageable to the entrepreneurs and easy to schedule meetings.

Advisory Board Member Profile

- People who can add strategic value to your business;

- People who think with you, but not necessarily like you;

- People with experience in a field you're not too good at;

- People who can give brutally frank feedback;

- People willing to share experience and insights;

- People who put the interests of the entrepreneur at the centre;

- People who are able to transcend their own professional background;

- People with good listening skills;

- People who are able to analyse things very quickly;

- People who are able to look out for what is missing;

- People who are battle-hardened;

- People who have the ability and willingness to commit time;

Note that an advisor need not necessarily be older than the entrepreneur.

Setting Up an Advisory Board

There is no real trick to recruiting advisors — you simply pitch them. Startups are cool these days, so most people are flattered by the request and are keen to be associated with a high-growth company. Phil Libin, cofounder and former CEO of Evernote, said that mentoring new entrepreneurs ultimately helped him become a better CEO.

- Screen for candidates who are truly motivated to help;

- Setting/managing expectations and roles up-front;

- Make it worth their while for them to stay involved;

Handling the Advisory Board

- Don't take feedback as either judgment or validation, but rather as a means to identify and prioritise risks and opportunities;

- It's still your job to own your business model;

- Don't look for opinions, but for solid, experience-based answers;

- If you don't agree—speak up;

- Opinions are not all that useful: it's experience that you want to leverage;

- Avoid small talk and focus on the business;

As a founder, you should be the leader of the advisory-board meeting. That's also why you need to stand up when you are present. Even if Advisory Board members are more knowledgeable in certain areas, there shouldn't be a student-teacher relationship. Be confident but coachable.

What an Advisory Board doesn't do:

- Babysit;

- Consult;

- Teach;

- Do the heavy lifting;

- Become window-dressing or an ego-booster;

- Become the public image of the company;

- Get operationally involved;

Like a startup valuation, getting
the right advisory board
is as much art as science.

"When the student is ready,
a teacher will appear."

— The Theosophical Society

Section 34
Pricing

Pricing Determines Your Market Position

Commitment of money is a powerful validation of your business model. The price your customers are willing to pay validates to what extent you have nailed the solution.

Pricing is one of the most sensitive topics in business. It will determine your market position, whether or not your customers will buy from you, the sales and distribution channels, and whether or not you're able to provide the standard of service expected by your customers.

Most of us set prices using competitive research and / or cost estimates. A high price may result in fewer customers, whereas a lower price might be seen as leaving money on the table.

Very often the price stays where it is, never knowing how many more customers you could have had or how much money you're leaving on the table. Price is the dominant factor for your profitability.

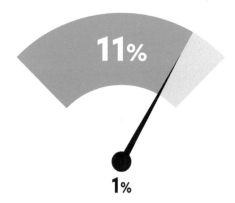

A price increase of 1% results in 11% increase in profit.

A Higher Price Means Fewer Customers

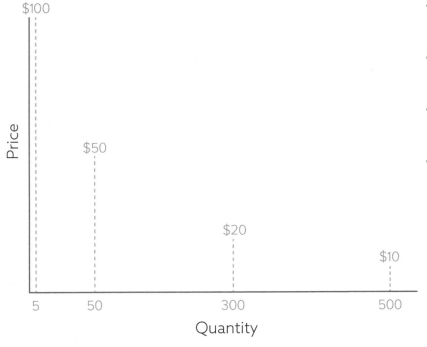

At a $ 10 price point:
500 customers will buy.

At a $ 20 price point:
300 customers will buy.

At a $ 50 price point:
50 customers will buy.

At a $ 100 price point:
5 customers will buy.

The Optimal Price-Customer Tandem

The optimal price will yield maximum revenue, not the highest margin or the largest number of customers.

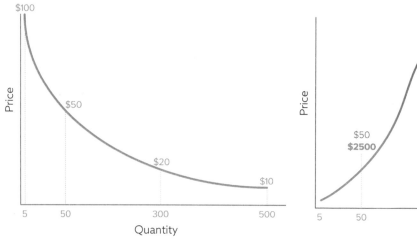

In economics, correlating price points with potential clients is known as the demand curve.

Multiply the number of potential clients with the respective price points to find the optimal price-customer tandem in order to maximise revenue.

Setting the Right Price

Price is not what you think you can charge, but what your customers are willing to pay based on the perceived value.

Traditionally, the price is the amount between cost and profit, which means that, in order to determine your profit, you need to subtract the cost from the price, which is known as lean thinking.

A better way to determine your profit is:
Sales – Fixed cost – Variable cost.

The better way for Startups to improve margins is to increase volume with the same fixed costs and lower variable costs. It should go without saying that the price must always be higher than costs.

Before setting the price, you need to ask yourself the right questions:

- Why would people pay for my services or products?

- What value will customers get from my offering?

Once you've identified why potential customers are willing to pay, you can create a business model to capture that value. In doing so, you need to have a clear understanding of your product's or service's value before you set the right price.

Deliver More than What the Customers Pay For

The value hierarchy is the structure of values that influences business decision-making.
Those values are:

- **Features:** A product's features represent the basic level of value delivered.

- **Advantage:** The advantages a product offers. This is a feature that competing products lack.

- **Benefit:** The benefit is the impact of your product on the customer's business, often measured as Return on Investment (ROI).

- **Benefit of the Benefit:** Ultimately, the decision-maker is a person who will take a risk by adopting your product at the organisation. Often it's important to understand what's in it for them in making the decision. This value is called the benefit of the benefit

- **The Pain of the Pain:** The pain of the pain is having a solution for a problem that is a pain in itself.

Increase revenue?
Decrease costs?
Reduce risk?
Save time?
Accelerate a process?
Provide non-monetary benefits?

What type of value are you delivering?
Make sure your product or service offers more than what the customers pay for.

Factors that Influence Pricing

For a trader, selling is buying. The purchase (input) cost drives 80 % of the sales price. For a manufacturer, selling is production-efficiency. The production cost drives 80 % of the sellling price.

For products based on Intellectual Property such as software, SaaS and web services, cost is driven by two major factors: the cost of sales and the level of support you intend to provide.

Value	Cost	Client Alternatives	Market
Need (B2C) vs. Pain (B2B)	Variable Cost	Doing nothing is #1 alternative	Type and Length of Contracts
Return on Investment (ROI)	Fixed Cost	Alternative is often the use of Excel	Competition
Must-Have vs. Nice-to-Have	Internal Cost Structure		Regulation

Remember to Revisit Pricing

Pricing is not a once-and-for-all, set-it-and-forget-it deal. Entering new markets, target different segments, inflation-index, new features, etc, can be reasons to revisit pricing.

A pricing strategy is a process that applies multiple tactics. Sadly, there is no "one-size-fits-all" answer when it comes to developing a pricing strategy. Pricing can be validated, but it can be done by no one other than yourself. Each paying customer is an achievement, so go and find out why they pay.

Make sure you don't over-engineer your pricing strategy, making it hard to understand. Pricing is also a function of marketing. Cash flow is as important as pricing, seeing that it's the only reason why business die.

Pricing is all about setting the right perception: water is more useful than a diamond, yet it is a lot cheaper.

The Dos and Don'ts of Pricing

DOs:

- Research the optimal price per customer in order to maximise revenue;

- Price is a continuous process;

- Understand why customer will pay you (value);

- Use industry gross margin as a starting point;

- Use tactics such as anchoring and decoy;

- Take into (margin) account the possibility of working with partners;

- Start with the premium part of freemium;

- Offer transactional pricing to transactional businesses only;

- Pricing is a function of marketing;

- Take Cash-flow into account;

DON'TS

- Set-it and forget-it;

- Cut prices in order to sell more;

- Overestimate Customer Lifetime Value;

- Ask clients for ballpark pricing;

- Underestimate the cost structure;

- Over-engineer or use more than three axes for pricing;

- Give discounts that aren't time-limited;

- Do pilots free of charge;

- Use freemium as a vanity metric;

- Subsidise the wrong side or both sides in a two-sided market model;

Section 35
Metrics & Analytics

The Importance of Metrics

Metrics are a standard of measurement to create accountability. Being accountable through metrics means making a commitment to a certain action. Perhaps the biggest challenge is to determine which metrics are actionable in order to steer the business in the right direction. Metrics can provide direction while also adding pressure on the team to perform.

The use of metrics at the product/market fit stage is rather qualitative: validating customer feedback, observing behaviour, etc. It's too soon to start extensive quantitative measurements if a product is not completely ready, or with too few or contradictory data points. A/B testing on almost nobody is simply a waste of time.

Bear in mind that a set of metrics is a simplistic representation of a complex reality. Keep your focus on your business, not the data. The more mature a business is, the more you can rely on numbers. For a startup, the numbers matter less than the quality of interactions with early adopters. Nothing can replace one-to-ones with early adopters to generate key insights.

Not All Metrics Are Created Equal

"A startup can focus on only one metric. So you have to decide which that is, and ignore the rest." (Noah Kagan)

While Kagan's advice is a way to make a point, it's true that you need to limit the number of metrics to focus on. Define the one or two key activities you think will drive use of the product. Think of one or two key indicators that your product is successful. Get insights into user behaviour: why are some happy, while others never come back? What distinguishes them?

Remember: measure what matters to your business and to your customers.

If the funnel is the key focus, use the Pirate Metrics from Dave McClure.

Acquisition How do users find you?

Activation Do users have a great first experience?

Retention Do users come back? ↓

Revenue How do you make money?

Referral Do users tell others?

The Importance of Metrics

Metrics are fun, but analytics kick ass. Analytics is the measurement of movement towards defined business goals, or when data are needed in order to answer a business question such as "What market segment generates the best traction?", "How to acquire new customers?" or "What new features are required?".

In general, good analytics are based on a ratio. For instance: the acquisition cost per customer; or they show a tension between two variables: ads shown versus bounce rate. Achieving a higher conversion rate is particularly important, as it indicates that the market likes what you have to offer.

Well-defined analytics keep you honest, and should even hurt. If you're not ashamed of some results, then something is wrong or you don't drill deep enough. Always call a spade a spade. Don't claim a retention rate of 95 % a month when in reality you're bleeding to death with an annual churn rate of 60 %. Or saying that you grow 50 percent week-on-week when you have only 5 customers and already lost 10. One needs to be particularly careful when using the freemium model; after all, having tons of users but only a few paying customers is hardly a sound basis for a sustainable business model.

In a startup, the ultimate purpose of analytics is to help you pivot and iterate your way towards product/market fit (before the cash runs out).

Pay special attention to outliers.
An exception doesn't prove the rule, it questions it.

If you keep doing what you're doing,
you'll keep getting what you're getting.

Data are like fish: they stink when they get old.

One paying customer is worth more than
1,000 likes on Facebook.

Lessons from House, MD

There are as many diagnostics as there are specialists.

Product-developers will tell you: "The product needs more features." while salespeople claim: "The product needs to be less technical." Everyone will see it from their own point of view.

Everybody tells lies

House doesn't believe everything his patients tell him: he only believes the symptoms. Similarly, you will hear "Of course I'll buy that!" from a prospect; "We'll be ready to ship in six months" from a developer and; "Of course I can sell that!" from a salesperson.

Tests take time, treatment is quicker

"We treat it. If he gets better, I'm right, if he dies, you're right." It's good advice to see whether your product or business is viable. In Daniel Kahneman's words, jumping to conclusions can be efficient if those conclusions are likely to be correct and the cost of an occasional mistake is acceptable.

* Source: Bruno Lowagie, iText http://itextpdf.com/houseMD

Taking Action

An alternative to the House MD approach is to build a continuous feedback loop with customers for rapid hypothesis-validation.

Use the feedback loop to:

- Start activities;

- Stop activities;

- Continue activities;

People who focus exclusively on efforts that matter will succeed. It's that simple.

"If you can't describe what you're doing as a process, you don't know what you're doing."

— Edwards Deming, Author

Section 36

Pivot

The Art of Pivoting

Pivoting is not the easiest decision to make. Yet pivots are the rule, not the exception, for companies that launch an innovative product or service for a new market. The key understanding of pivoting is that a startup cannot change course completely. The existing team, work already done, development effort, lessons learned and knowledge gathered would limit such freedom. You pivot when you see notice some aspect of a business model gets way more traction than what you had assumed in the hypothesis. Or you receive feedback or observe behaviour from customers who expressed different needs. Thus, a pivot is not a leap into the unknown. Leaping is when you don't have anything to stick with, and want to start again from scratch. Since you can't predict the number of pivots required to reach product/market fit, you can't impose a deadline on it.

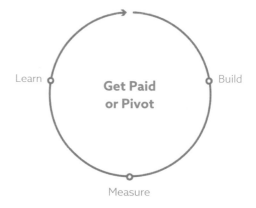

Also, it's likely that in the broad domain of problems or needs that the startup is trying to solve, the seed of a pivot is hidden. Pivots are rooted in learning what works and what doesn't, leaving "one foot in the past" and "one foot in a possible new future," Ries says. Pivots are based on insights, regrouping and rethinking with an open mind. Pivoting is a reconfiguration of resources and business models with the aim of renewing the creation, distribution and capture of value. From that perspective, Marc Andreessen's notorious statement on pivots is at least open to question: The pivot. It used to be called, 'the fuck-up.' Philosopher Nietzsche summarised it best: "Many are stubborn in pursuit of the path they have chosen. Few are in pursuit of the goal."

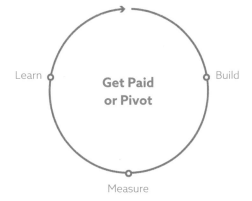

Effectuation

The effectuation framework can help to make a pivot decision and move from that point onwards, using the following principles:

 Bird-in-hand: who we are, what we know, what we have and whom we know. Imagine the possibilities that originate from the means.

 Crazy Quilt: obtain pre-commitments from stakeholders to reduce uncertainty and co-create new markets.

 Affordable Loss: limit risk by knowing how much you can afford to lose.

 Pilot-in-the-plane: focus on activities that are within your control

 Lemonade: use core insights as potential clues to create new markets or business models.

Pivot is a change of strategy, business model or product, not necessarily a change of vision

Visions rarely change: strategies change regularly, while products change constantly. So a pivot is not when you fire the whole team and start a new company from scratch based on a new vision or idea.

vision

Strategy

Business Model / Product

Types of Pivot

- A single feature becomes the product

- The product becomes a feature

- Shifting from B2B to B2C or vice-versa

- Value-creation pivot

- Value-distribution pivot

- Value-capturing pivot

- Technology shift

- Customer segment/market pivot

Some great companies came out of Pivots:

"So, verily, with every difficulty, there is relief."

— Holy Quran

Section 37
Winding Down

How Do You Know When to Fold?

Contrary to the aphorism "Winners never quit and quitters never win", successful people know when it's time to stop persisting and start quitting. Stop spending valuable time projecting and protecting the initial vision. You simply can't impose an idea whose time hasn't yet come.

We've all been in situations in which the right choice is anything but clear. How do you know when to carry on, or make the call to stop? After all, the most valuable resource you have is your time, and if it's wasted on a dead end, you can never get that time back. If everything you do to try to breathe life into your product is without effect, the time has come to move on. The earlier the startup is in its lifecycle, the easier it is to walk away. Take care of the wounded and bury the dead, not vice-versa.

It is tough to deal with the social consequences of the onset of failure. Exploring the point at which a startup accepts that giving up is the only option left will reveal much about founders. Perhaps the best thing to do at this point is to ask yourself how you can help people more. In that sense, quitting is just a pivot in one's life. For every door that closes, another will open.

Define Success Criteria

It helps to set success criteria, and if you fail to hit those criteria, then you really need to assess whether or not you're still on the right track. Trying and failing is useful if there is a consistent direction, but if the goals change every month, each failure will lead to starting from the beginning, over and over again. That is hardly progress.

Give yourself a clear set of milestones to achieve, then set a few deadlines that you need to hit these minimum milestones, or else you will leave. This could be revenue, users, funding, cash in the bank or some other key milestone that is essential for the viability of the company. Tell your cofounders and team the deadlines you are attaching to key milestones. This will provide the motivation and pressure to focus on those milestones.

Success criteria can be rational and external, such as the number of paying customers. If one can have 10 paying customers, getting to 100 is likely. Once you have 100, what can prevent you from reaching 1,000? Break it down into orders of magnitude.

You can easily set up some reasonable criteria, but rationality is not everything. You can also use internal signals. If the team has lost faith in the idea; if every morning you need to force yourself out of bed; if the atmosphere feels deeply unhappy and team members are starting to blame each other, etc. Usually the rational success criteria and internal signals are connected. If they are not, i.e. you have failed the success criteria, but the team is in the flow, be persistent. That's why stopping is more art than science.

"The temptation to quit will be greatest just before you are about to succeed."

— Old Chinese proverb

About the Author

Omar Mohout, Partner & Head of Digital at Nova Reperta, is a former technology entrepreneur, a widely published technology author, C-level advisor to high growth startups as well as Fortune 500 companies and Professor of Entrepreneurship at Antwerp Management School and Solvay Brussels School of Economics and Management.

Mohout is Chairman of BeCentral, the largest digital skills campus in Europe; Advisory Board member of the Euronext TechShare Program; member of the Advisory Boards for Digital Transformation Conference and Internet of Things Convention, Advisor to the AI4Belgium board, advisor to the State Secretary for Digitalization and; Advisory Board member at Stellar Labs. He also joined the Board of Directors of venture capital fund imec. iStart.

Mohout is a keynote speaker and panelist on digital transformation at leading conferences.

Other Books by the Author

About Nova Reperta

Set up in 2011 by seasoned consultants and managers sharing an entrepreneurial drive. And that drive is still there, but we're now part of a team of about 50+ professionals obsessively focused on creating impact with our clients. That goal attracts ambitious, entrepreneurial people who naturally combine soft and hard skills. And that immediately evokes the five core values that tie us together: entrepreneurial, pragmatic, inclusive, trustworthy and always exploring.

Nova Reperta helps your company to set a clear course for success and cultivate the strategies, processes, tools and mindset you need. So you can do more with the same. Put your customer at the heart of everything you do. Cherish your human capital. And do it fast.

That is how our ~50 consultants transform this mission (almost) impossible into an adventure for your organization. One that paves the way to new solutions, new markets, new revenue streams and new opportunities for profit and growth.

Don't just take it from us. Check out our website on www.novareperta.com and discover what our clients say about us, what we stand for and how we make it work. Enjoy!